From Data to Insights

John Mackay

From Data to Insights

The Strategy of a Data Analytics Team

 Springer

John Mackay
Auchterarder, UK

ISBN 978-981-96-3544-3   ISBN 978-981-96-3545-0   (eBook)
https://doi.org/10.1007/978-981-96-3545-0

This Springer imprint is published by the registered company Springer Nature Singapore Pte Ltd.
The registered company address is: 152 Beach Road, #21-01/04 Gateway East, Singapore 189721,
Singapore

If disposing of this product, please recycle the paper.

Preface

This is a handbook for building a data analytics team.

There are many variations of data analytics teams, different scopes, requirements, industries and sizes. All data analytics teams follow a similar journey in developing their capabilities, whether the team is small or large, works with executive, operational, financial, regulatory, or forecasting, and whether your outputs are reporting, insight, or analysis.

This book takes a practical approach, guiding you through logical steps to help you define and implement a strategy for building or transforming your team.

Throughout this book, the terms data analytics, business intelligence (BI), analytics reporting, and management information (MI) will be used interchangeably. Whilst there are nuances between them, the underlying roles these functions serve are aligned, and the steps to build these teams are the same.

In the later sections of this book, there are chapters dealing with specific functions, such as data science or AI, which may or may not be relevant to your team. This book is modular, allowing readers to skip any subchapter as needed, as long as the four key elements of team, data, stakeholders, and reporting are addressed. We will explain these four elements in detail throughout this book.

This book is structured to progress through these four elements in this order, as this is the order in which you should approach the creation of your strategy.

We will start this process by discussing what we do on the first day and then use this to start building the goals that form our long-term strategy.

Within the leadership and team chapters, we will take a look at ourselves and the teams we have and will create, building on our strengths and supporting team development.

Following this, we will look at the data our team will work with, how it is sourced, processed, and other considerations, such as architectures, products, and other features of our data we must regard.

Next, we will consider our stakeholders, including how we interact with them, the key questions we need to ask, and what not to ask.

Reporting is the final element of our strategic goals that we will address, covering many of the major tools used in data analytics. Don't worry though, the concept of all visualisation tools is very similar. Once you know one, the rest are incredibly easy to pick up.

Finally, we will work through how to collate our strategic goals that we have built throughout this book and create a strategic plan to achieve these goals.

The application of this book remains the same whether you are a CTO, director, manager, team lead, or member of a data or analytics team. For data and analytics practitioners, even if you are not responsible for delivering the strategy of your team, understanding how a strategy is shaped and the elements that form it is essential for delivering great outputs.

Most data analytics teams suffer from a combination of these issues:

1. Too many ad hoc requests
2. Poor reliability and reputation
3. Not enough time spent on analysis and insight
4. Urgent last-minute requests
5. Inconsistent and hard-to-use reports
6. Unhappy colleagues with no drive
7. Stakeholders having to make their own reporting

All of these are caused by poor strategy and design, and very few teams manage to operate without a number of these problems.

A reporting team most often follows one of the two routes. Either struggling to cope with reporting demands or having so much red-tape it becomes irrelevant to the business it supports.

Sometimes, a defining failure can stem from one poor decision made early on in the creation of a team's strategy, or even from the lack of a strategy, or the inability to follow one. More often than not, failure is caused by a lack of understanding of what the manager should be aiming for and on what journey the strategy should take them on.

This book will fix that.

Auchterarder, UK   John Mackay

Contents

About the Author

John Mackay is a seasoned data analytics manager with a passion for building data analytics teams that provide actionable insights to drive strategic decisions, improve the business, and create supportive and engaging teams. With over two decades of experience, John has perfected his skills in creating innovative strategies, building and leading high-performing teams, and delivering value through data.

John Mackay started his career in the world of finance, working for one of the largest banking groups in Europe. John has extensive experience in data analytics, having held various roles within a team, including data engineer, data manager, project manager, and reporting and analytics analysis and management, before building and leading his own teams.

With this full range of data and analytics skills, John developed and implemented comprehensive data infrastructures, reporting suites, and analytics platforms that significantly improved operational efficiency and compliance.

Through these teams, John has undertaken a range of responsibilities, including regulatory, transactional, financial, operational, forecasting, and executive reporting, covering every aspect of data analytics. These teams have achieved substantial cost and FTE savings, delivering millions of pounds in savings and billions of pounds in customer benefits.

Currently, as the group manager of data analytics at a leading technology firm, John leads several analytics teams. Through this company, John also provides consultancy services to Fortune 500 companies and has developed data products for Tech 50 companies, yielding substantial results for both the companies and their customers.

Chapter 1
Introduction: Day 1 Strategy

The first days of managing a data analytics team are challenging.

The obvious comes first. Speak to your manager(s). Speak to your team. Ask questions, ask for opinions, and don't have preconceived ideas. Stakeholder introductions come next.

It is all too easy to accept the existing ways of working, or suggestions from stakeholders and other team members on what should be worked on and how.

Your focus must be on identifying both the positives and negatives of the way the team is operating. Whilst doing this you need to think about where you want the team to be and how it should operate.

The delta between where a team is at now and where it needs to be is usually huge. Starting to build a strategy for your team is challenging. Knowing where to start and what to focus on.

Working out what journey to take your team on, what changes need implementing and what you are going to spend your next year working on is NOT what you want to start with.

Working out the small changes, or immediate issues to tackle is also NOT what you want to start with.

The immediate priorities you will be handed by your senior leaders, by your team, and even by the previous manager are important, but having a primary focus on these will stop you from thinking about how to transform the team. Most of the time these priorities will be so urgent, precisely because the team is not functioning optimally and doesn't have the right framework and capabilities to be able to deliver them quickly and effectively.

We will discuss extensively how we decide what we need to work on first and why, as this is one of the key changes we need to make in our approach to managing a data and analytics team.

J. Mackay, *From Data to Insights*, https://doi.org/10.1007/978-981-96-3545-0_1

Your day 1 strategy should be to pause any major or transformational changes and maintain business as usual (BAU) whilst you develop a long-term strategy.

It is imperative that our primary focus should be: thinking about what you want the end goals of the team to look like.

1.1   Long-Term Focus

It is natural to attempt to identify what can be worked on first; ways of freeing up the team, removing manual steps, so that you can then generate some time in the team, which can then be used to further develop the team. It is the way most managers will start.

It sounds sensible, but it does not work.

Short-term strategy without long-term goals very rarely works as planned. These interim measures are likely to take longer than expected and often leave the team processes, reporting or infrastructure in a more complex situation, which will then take even longer to transform into your end strategy.

For more detail, and many more reasons to avoid short-term strategy, as this is such an important subject, later on in this book is a chapter dedicated to "Quick-Wins" (Sect. 8.4).

Instead, we must focus on long-term goals. The dilemma you may encounter initially, is that you don't know what your long-term goals should be, so instead should you get your team working on short-term goals until you fully understand the full picture?

This is when you have to ensure your focus is on long-term strategy and improvement in how the team is working. This way, we can ensure the decisions being made not only by yourself, but the whole team are ones that are progressing your team and not just treading water.

To span the gap of focussing on the immediate issues against delivering a long-term strategy, we can start by drawing up a day 1 strategy, that will be a work-in-progress that we can revisit and adapt continually as we learn and understand more about the team and its challenges.

1.2   Business Goals

The end goals you decide on should be aspirational. They will be used to guide your team development, inspire your team to think strategically, and motivate them.

Goals that support your business, and can demonstrate how your engineers and analysts are helping the business, customers or the public, are the ones that inspire the most. These goals are the ones your senior leadership will want to hear about and the ones that will be on the sales brochure of your team.

It can at times be hard to see how your data and analytics team will provide these wider benefits. Here are a few examples of what types of goals you might have for a range of different data and analytics teams:

1. Protect customers from fraud through better controls.
2. Simplify the reporting suite for the business to make it easier to understand the environment.
3. Build great customer insight through new tools and data science.
4. Create predictive analytics to understand the future.
5. Use robotics and AI to remove manual tasks for operational colleagues.
6. Evolve our planning capability.
7. Improve the decisions we make for our customers.
8. Provide better tools for colleagues when they are engaging with customers.
9. Empower our colleagues with better tools.

These are all great goals for the team, and this type of goals will help inspire your team and senior leadership.

However, these goals are not very good for a strategy for the actions you need to take and implement in your data and analytics team.

For the purpose of this book, we will think of these as *Business Goals.*

What we need to do is translate these into *Data and Insight Goals* (Sect. 1.3).

1.3   Data and Insight Goals

Data and insight goals differ from business goals, in that these need to be actionable tasks that describe exactly what is going to be happening. This means they need to be low level rather than high level, and address specific changes that need to be enacted.

The two elements of a data and analytics team that are most often focussed on by their management are the requests of **senior stakeholders** and the **visuals of their reporting**. Throughout this book, we will explain and demonstrate why these are two of the least important aspects to focus on.

This will however, cause an issue. What is expected of your team from many senior managers will usually not align to what actually needs working on. This becomes ever more obvious, when senior managers have a lack of business or technical knowledge, or understanding of how data works.

Perhaps you are working in a business in which you are fortunate enough to have knowledgeable and experienced leaders, but if you are not, then communication of what you have learned and a demonstration of this in practice will be key to challenging the culture of your business.

The goals will align to the four elements of a reporting team:

1. Team (Chap. 3)
2. Data (Chap. 4)
3. Stakeholders (Chap. 7)
4. Reporting and Insight (Chap. 8)

For some inspiration, here is a list of goals that might apply:

- A cross-skilled team with no knowledge gaps.
- A happy and productive team.
- Interactive reporting to end users can explore trends.
- 100% automation of reporting. No-one likes manual reporting.
- All new reports peer checked by two other colleagues and signed off by stakeholders.
- In-built insight and call-outs.
- One page/tab reporting, let's get rid of 20-page reports.
- Multi-functional reporting. Combine daily/weekly/monthly, different products and categories onto one report dynamically.
- No more ad-hoc reporting due to really comprehensive reporting.
- Proactively create reporting capabilities before they are asked for.
- Deliver a new visualisation tool.
- Customer insight.
- Create a new infrastructure.
- Accessible documentation and definitions for every report and metric.
- Weekly engagement with stakeholders to discuss changes to the business and reporting.

Each goal you pick for your team will have its own journey. Some of your goals will be dependent on others, some will be quick to achieve and some may even take years.

Before you move on to the next step, I would like you to revisit the goal you have decided on. The chances are, you have not focussed enough on the data.

The four elements of a reporting team mentioned previously are all important, but not equally so. The order listed is the order of importance.

1. Team—The whole team needs to be taken on the journey of your strategy. They need to be motivated by what the manager is trying to achieve, and embrace the ideals. Then they can see the benefits and deliver a solution that will last, and not just lapse back into previous habits.
2. Data—Without a great infrastructure you will never have great reporting. Creating a report should be 90% data development, 10% report building.
3. Stakeholders—Stakeholder engagement will be key to fully delivering your strategy. If your goals don't align with what your stakeholders needs, then these goals cannot succeed.
4. Reporting—Reporting relies on the three previous elements being in place. Without any one of these, this element will fail.

1.4   Chapter Summary

1. Start by speaking to your managers, team and find out the positives and negatives of the way the team is operating.
2. Pause any major or transformational changes.
3. Maintain BAU whilst you develop a long-term strategy.

Chapter 2
Leadership

2.1 Protection

The team manager or director should be the face of the team and the primary interface into senior leadership. Don't gloss over this. The team manager must protect the pressure of senior leadership from the team. Whilst visibility for colleagues is a great development opportunity, it is upon the team manager to prevent the pressure of competing priorities from both senior management and senior stakeholders.

Failure to do this is incredibly common and results in teams that chase their tails endlessly never create the initially envisaged infrastructure and end up with one giant cottage industry.

Cottage industry—A localised process that is highly manual, time intensive, usually run by one person, often pulling a few data sources into files saved locally or on a desktop, and creating unreliable outputs.

Both senior leadership and senior stakeholders will ask for temporary solutions and quick-wins. Once you go down this route, your strategy will fail. Equally, constant requirement changes and additional-asks will do the same. There are dedicated chapters to these subjects later in this book.

2.2 Responsibility and Knowledge

Similar to offering protection to the team, the manager is also responsible to ensure that the framework and ethos is of the team functions well. Failures in data and analytics teams are often blamed on the colleague who directly created the fault, however with a better framework in place, this fault would have been impossible, or at least spotted and resolved.

The later chapters in this book cover this in detail, but before we get to that, we need to understand why responsibility and knowledge are intertwined.

On the 4th June 1996, the unmanned Ariane V 501 space rocket prepared to launch. The rocket carried a $500 Million cargo and was to be the first commercial flight in this $7 Billion programme (Fig. 2.1).

Thirty-nine seconds after take-off, the rocket exploded in a fireball.

The cause of this was a conversion error between a 64 bit and 32 bit field.

Quite simply, a field in the system was expecting a number less than 32,768, but after 36.7 seconds of flight, a larger number was received.

Investigations followed, finding the management of the project largely to be at fault, in this disaster which cost the European Space Agency a further $1.15 Billion [1].

Initially the blame might be placed on the requirements gathering for the module that errored, or the stakeholder engagement, or collaboration between teams. Potentially the coders making an error, or very likely the testers and insufficient testing.

Fortunately, the French investigators were thorough.

What Was This Module That Failed? It was a system to detect lateral motion prior to take-off. It wasn't even needed in-flight, but a time/cost saving decision was made to leave it on for the duration of the flight.

Fig. 2.1 Ariane V (https:// pixabay.com/photos/ toulouse-space-city-rocket- ariane-5-6592033/)

How Did It Fail? Usually, a program would have error catching to restart a process if there is a problem and deal with it. But again, a time/cost saving decision was made to leave this out on such a simple module.

How Did This Pass Testing? The module had been tested thoroughly, but on a previous rocket, the Ariane IV. Once again, a time/cost saving decision was made not to retest the module that had previously been so reliable.

The investigating team found the management of the Ariane project at fault in two areas.

1. It was the environment, frameworks, and processes that the management had put into place that had failed. It was their responsibility to facilitate this.
2. There had been insufficient technical understanding in the management. Without the understanding of what was important, they had been unable to ensure the right focus was in place.

The issues faced by the Ariane project are comparable to the ones you will encounter in your team. As a manager you will both need to have enough knowledge of the detail of your team's work, and what, who, and when to delegate decisions.

2.3 Technical Expertise

Technical expertise is far too often overlooked in management, in favour of leadership-skills and stakeholder management.

Although a manager can succeed without knowledge of how a database, tables, views, and reports work, it is almost always to the detriment of the team. Lack of this knowledge results in under-appreciation of what is involved technically in each stage of a strategy, and a misplaced focus in all elements of the team.

Typically, this will result in managers who focus on the end product and making the final report look pretty, with little attention paid to the 95% of the infrastructure that should have been the primary focus.

Leadership-skills and stakeholder management are extremely important for a manager, but are equal to the knowledge of how and what the team will be building.

> We would not put a pilot in the cockpit without extensive flight training; why would we expect someone with no IT experience to be close to successful? They do not know what to execute on or what to prioritise which leads to endless risk reduction efforts and diluted focus. IT is a highly skilled and trained job; Staff it as such.
> —Nicolas M. Chaillan. U.S. Air Force & Space Force Chief Software Officer (CSO) [2]

It is the processes that we as leaders put into place, that define how our team's work.

If you are hiring a manager, ensure they have this expertise. If you are this manager, then start learning. None of these skills are unsurmountable. Even a basic understanding of the coding languages, table structures and reporting elements you will be utilising will be invaluable.

2.4   Delegation

Rather than delegation of tasks to your team or other teams, this is the delegation of decisions and strategy.

The manager of a good team will seek advice from the most experienced colleagues they can for every major decision. Sometimes you will be the most experienced, but the humility to know when you are not, is a hurdle is one we must cross.

Quite often senior managers will create reports, design reports, decide how data is brought in and structured. More often than not they will have team members who have far superior expertise in this, and not realise the mistakes they are making and will not end up with the best product.

Whilst not literally for a reporting team, *what you don't know can kill you* (Fig. 2.2).

This matrix is one that I have often referenced to explain the realm of the "Things we don't know we don't know", which is the most dangerous part of anyone's working life.

How can we fix or carry out things we don't know even exist?

This is why we need to ensure we seek advice from the right expert in each field and not think we have more knowledge than we actually have.

		Our Perceived Knowledge	
		Known	Unknown
Real State of Knowledge	Known	Things we know we know	Things we don't know we know
	Unknown	Things we know we don't know	Things we don't know we don't know

Fig. 2.2 Donald Rumsfeld's matrix of epistemic uncertainty [3]

However, we can work to reduce the "Things we don't know we don't know". By learning more about everything we can within the world we work in, we can expand out the areas we know, reducing the areas we don't know.

> The frontier of discovery is a messy place... You don't know what is true. You don't even know what questions to ask necessarily. Maybe you think you know what question to ask, and it's the wrong question...
> As the area of our knowledge grows, so too does the perimeter of our ignorance
> —Neil deGrasse Tyson, Astrophysicist [4]

Many managers are well aware of not understanding what their team does, and leaving decisions entirely to them. This is vastly limiting. By doing this, the manager will not understand the consequences of other decisions they are making within a team.

Learning a coding language or application to the level of your engineers may take years. Though this level of knowledge would be great, it is not necessary. We just need to get the level of our knowledge to the point where we understand the concepts of everything being carried out by the team.

Learn and develop your own skills, and use this to be able to ask the right questions and seek the right expertise from your team.

A little knowledge can be a bad thing, but it is far better than not understanding at all.

Example: Not Delegating and "Things We Don't Know We Don't Know"

A new manager of an existing team that was swamped with manual processes and new requests, set out to reduce their workload.

This new manager understood that automation of the existing BAU reporting would give the team more time to start working on a new strategy.

Automation was something they understood.

One of the team members suggested that instead of automating reporting first, they should focus on improving the underlying data structures, as each report was using different logic and different underlying data.

This idea did not seem to offer any immediate benefit.

The new manager also had no understanding of data structures, how the reporting used the data or how any of the logic or processing for this worked.

For them, everything before the report was an unknown. They knew they did not know how the data for a report was brought into is and how this logic worked.

So, the new manager directed the engineers to start work on automation, which they expected to be complete within weeks.

This automation dragged on for over 6 months. The engineers were able to automate the reports, but then were finding that because the underlying data between the reports was different, when they came to test the reporting, nothing ever matched. Therefore, they would then have to go back to the source data and fix this, then start again with the automation.

In this situation here is where the realms of knowledge laid for the new manager: Fig. 2.3.

This new manager failed to either delegate the decision to the experts. Or to learn about and understand how the data infrastructure for the team worked.

There was too much that the new manager didn't know that they didn't know. If they would have understood the importance of having a reliable, comprehensive data source for all reporting that comes from the same source, either through delegating that decision, or learning the subject themselves, then the decision would have been different.

| | | Our Perceived Knowledge | |
		Known	Unknown
Real State of Knowledge	Known	(1) Automation.	(2) -
	Unknown	(3) Where reporting data comes from	(4) The data structures and different data sources

Fig. 2.3 Donald Rumsfeld's matrix of epistemic uncertainty in use

2.5   Chapter Summary

1. Data and analytics teams fail because the frameworks the colleagues are working in are not robust enough. It is the responsibility of the team manager to ensure these frameworks are sufficient and effective.
2. Leaders need to understand the fundamentals of what is happening in their teams. This will help you to make better decisions, and also to know when and who to delegate decisions to.
3. You need to know data. Whatever your role. If your company/organisation uses data (and it does), then you need to understand what is going on and why.
4. Would you fly in an aircraft captained by someone that doesn't know how to fly?

References

1. *A Bug and a Crash*. James Gleick, New York Times Magazine (1996) https://www-users.cse. umn.edu/~arnold/disasters/a-bug-and-a-crash.pdf
2. *It is time to say Goodbye*! Nicolas M. Chaillan. U.S. Air Force & Space Force Chief Software Officer (CSO) (2021) https://www.linkedin.com/pulse/time-say-goodbye-nicolas-m-chaillan
3. *Donald Rumsfeld's Matrix of Epistemic Uncertainty*. Donald Rumsfeld. United States Secretary of Defense (2009) https://en.wikipedia.org/wiki/There_are_known_knowns
4. *Surviving in Space without a Spacesuit*. Neil deGrasse Tyson, Astrophysicist. (2015) https:// ed.ted.com

Chapter 3
Building a Team

3.1 Roles: Who to Hire?

Whether you are transforming an existing team, or building a new one, you will need to consider the number of staff you will have available for this team and their roles.

In many reporting teams, the roles of the team are blurred, and team members find themselves out of their comfort zone, working on activities they did not expect and were not suited for. Over time as the team evolves the roles we have and roles we need diverge.

3.1.1 The Role of the Database Administrator (DBA)

The DBA will be responsible for designing and creating the technical infrastructure for your team.

You will need a DBA if you are working with a fresh server install, or need a major redesign of an existing server infrastructure. Their responsibilities include:

- Installation, management, and administration of a server.
- Modification of database structures.
- Allocating and monitoring system storage.
- Monitoring and optimisation of server performance.
- Implementing user management.
- Ensuring potential backup and recovery of server structure/data.
- Implementing archiving and audit processes.
- Ensure optimised import and structures for incoming data.
- Act as SME for data queries.

3.1.2   The Role of the Senior Engineer

The senior engineer will have many of the same skills as the DBA, usually without the same level of certification and experience.

The senior engineer will be responsible for creating tables and views within the server, optimising and managing these, and ensuring the successful day-to-day running of the server.

They may also have line manager responsibility for engineers.

3.1.3   The Role of the Engineer

Engineers will usually be on the route to progressing to a senior engineer and will have a great working knowledge of the coding languages required, though likely without the understanding of all the administration processes involved in database and server management.

Their focus will be in creating data import mechanisms/pipelines, and where requires transforming this into data the analysts can work with.

3.1.4   The Role of the Analyst and Senior Analyst

These roles should focus on manipulating and transforming the data provided to create dashboards and insight.

They will carry out report maintenance, stakeholder engagement, insight, presentation, analysis, and ad-hoc reporting.

This role is a technical one, and analysts are expected to know both the database languages and visualisation tools.

Within the database, analysts will often create routines for data transformation.

Senior analysts may have more technical experience, but should still work closely with engineers when designing technical solutions in the creation of reports. They usually also have line manager responsibility for other report analysts.

Report analysts are essential in executive reporting teams, where analysis and insight will be a key focus.

3.1.5   The Role of the Data Scientist

The role of a data scientist can crossover with the roles of an engineer and of an analyst.

Both a data scientist and an engineer will interrogate raw data, manipulate data and try to assemble data in the right way for future use, though the data manipulation undertaken by the data scientist will often be one-off pieces of work, which when completed may be passed back to an engineer to adapted for regular production.

Both a data scientist and an analyst will take data to carry out analysis and insight, though an analyst will focus on creating dashboards to illustrate key metrics and support the business, whilst the data scientist will focus on advanced analysis to create actionable insights.

This might involve activities such as predictive models, machine learning, natural language processing, or advanced analysis, which are explained in the Sect. 6.3 later in this book.

3.2 Recruitment

When we are recruiting for new colleagues, it is important to set clear expectations and not to set too wide a scope for their skillset.

3.2.1 Conflicting Skills Required

Nearly every role will have a set of essential skills and preferable skills to have. Many of these will be generic, some will be pointless (*everyone thinks they are a self-motivated, enthusiastic, passionate, team player with attention to detail and a proactive mind-set*), some will define the specific tools being used or set the scene for what skills will form the daily routine.

We should expect a job description to focus on one of the roles described in the Sect. 3.1. There may often be a blend of two of these roles. In this case, we should focus on the day-to-day activities of this position and identify which is the primary role we are focussing on.

Perhaps the position description is looking for a senior reporting analyst/manager to present regular insight to very senior management, whilst also looking for specific technical database development skills to transform the way data is brought in and stored for that team. This tells us that the scope of the role is realistically going to be too large for one person, and so the goals of the hiring manager are not likely to be achievable.

3.2.2 Too Many Technical Skills Required

A frequent problem with vacancy descriptions is an unrealistic list of systems and technical skills a candidate must possess.

An example of this is an analytics manager role looking for the candidate to be proficient in SQL, SAS, R, Python, Tableau, Power BI, and Excel. Then to preferably have skills in PowerShell, Bash, and a range of company specific data sources.

These requirements are indicative of a role in which the responsibilities are not clearly defined, a hiring manager not understanding the similarity between tools and languages, or possibly just a poorly written advert.

Later on in this book, in the Sect. 6.8, we will talk more around conversion between different tools and languages.

3.2.3 Qualifications Against Experience

Qualifications are great, the more up to date and relevant the better. We do need to be careful that qualifications are from reputable sources, and that there has been value in undertaking the courses, whether this is looking through resumes or looking for qualifications to undertake ourselves.

Experience is also great. Many skills that are invaluable and even essential to employees aren't taught at universities or by course providers. Even when these are taught, putting them into practice is when the learning actually starts, the course just gave us the tools to start learning.

A substantial proportion of engineers are self-taught. This can be both weakness and strength. Undertaking a course in development, such as a Microsoft Certified Azure Qualification will give a holistic view of everything related to development. However, much of it will be irrelevant, and some really core concepts are barely touched on and the vast importance not really mentioned (such as indexes, which are the backbone of performant databases).

A self-taught engineer can be one that has learned the bare minimum to carry out their role, or they could be one that has continuously developed themselves and will try to learn more and more skills and techniques as they progress. This generally becomes evident in a comparison of how long they have been carrying out this role, and what recent tools and languages they have in their skillset.

There isn't a correct answer for this, a blend of qualifications and experience is usually what we are looking for.

However, there is a wrong answer. A good number of vacancies for data and analytics roles look for industry specific qualifications. Whether this is an accountancy qualification for an engineer role, or a mathematics qualification for a reporting analyst. In doing this, we so severely limit our pool of prospective candidates that we are likely to be left with people who have very little experience in the job they will actually be doing. Would having an accountancy or mathematics degree really help designing the infrastructure, and improving the performance of a database? Section 6.8 discusses this more later in the book.

When hiring a manager, it can be harder to assess exactly what type of experience the candidate has. An MBA is one of the few manager-specific qualifications available; however, it is somewhat generic, and an MBA from a less reputable university may not prove very challenging. A BSC/MSC in digital and technology solutions is a clear indication the candidate will have detailed knowledge of data; however, this needs to be backed up with evidence that they have not only managed a data team, but really understand the data. It is also likely to be quite rare to find a manager with this qualification, and a lack of qualifications like this should not be a blocker [1].

3.3 Specialisation Vs Cross-Skilling

Just as most organisations will yo-yo between reporting departments being aligned with operational/business areas to better understand their customers, and reporting departments being centralised so expertise, experience and best practice can be shared; so, a conundrum exists within the reporting team of whether to have the whole team skilled in everything, or having specialised colleagues for each area.

Should team members specialise in areas, so they can build up such knowledge as to be an SME and be able to offer the best possible customer service in that area, or should a team be entirely cross skilled so there is never a risk of having a skill gap from colleague absence.

With specialisation, colleagues get a better sense of ownership. Conversely, working in this silo prevents them developing other skills as easily.

With specialisation, colleagues get to build great relationships with customers. Conversely, a strained relationship between clashing personalities had cause havoc.

With cross-skilling, colleagues get the opportunity to develop across a broader spectrum. Conversely, they might become a jack of all trades and master of none.

Risk is mitigated by everyone being able to do everything. However, every change takes longer because no-one has a full understanding of the data/processes/reporting, so lengthy investigation is required.

Fortunately, there are ways to do both. The problem started before we even answered the question. This comes from your perspective of the issue. By focussing about the end results, we have ignored the root cause. The root cause is in the data.

If the data for every specialisation is defined in a standard way, tables named logically, fields named logically, calculations performed as early to the source data as possible, and in scripts/views on the server rather than in report code, then it becomes much easier to understand each area.

Logical and insightful table/view naming and table structure *(the schema of the database)* allow engineers and analysts to focus on the end product and the customer rather than trying desperately to understand how something is calculated.

One other important aspect of specialisation and cross-skilling is how well the team can cope with leavers and absence. The more a team specialises or finds it difficult for team members to be able to pick up tasks they don't regularly work with, the less it is able to mitigate team members leaving, or absences.

3.4   Team Structure

The drivers for the structure of your team will be in the work they are carrying out. However, it is key to bear in mind that the work of the team will change. The team's initial goals of creating the new strategy are likely to change once the initial development is complete and your target infrastructure embedded.

There are no rules or formulae to work out the numbers of staff in each role you will need, so instead you will need to draft out what you think will be required for the initial transformation of the team, and what you think will be required for the BAU running of the team once this is complete.

Example: Team Structure Implementation Scenarios

Scenario 1: Creating a start-up operational reporting team

Reporting type	Operational	Permanent FTE	5
Data tool	SQL server	Contractor FTE	2
Reporting tool	Excel	Contractor tenure	6 months

Remit: Provide telephony, quality, and complaint operational reporting with a 6-month lead time.

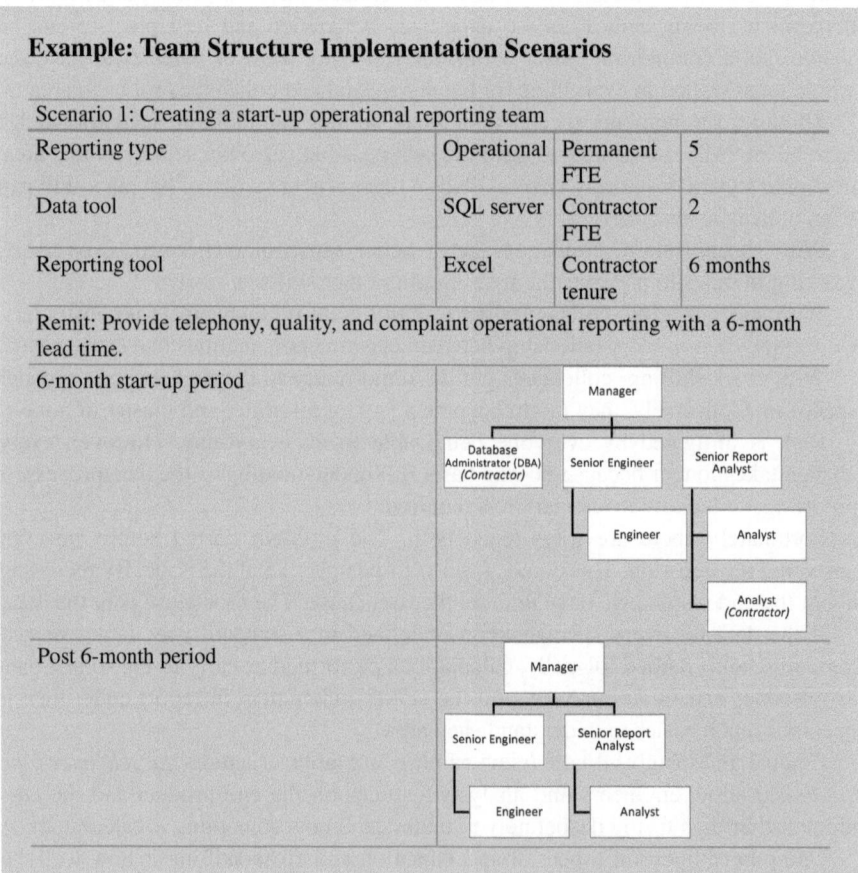

Scenario 1: Creating a start-up operational reporting team

Technical strategy: Three reporting areas need to be reported on. Each one will need imports from the source systems, then tables and views created on the SQL server.
The team will be split functionally into engineers and reporting.
Initially the role of the reporting team will be to gain requirements from the operation, whilst the development team will focus on creating the infrastructure.
After the build of the tables, the reporting team will provide the requirements of how the SQL views need to be created, from which the reporting team can start work on creating the reports.
As this reporting is created, the development team will then focus on automation and other required tasks such as user access, logging, audit requirements, etc.
Each reporting area will take 3 months to create, split roughly:
30% requirements gathering.
50% infrastructure development.
20% report creation.
These periods will need to be staggered, and careful planning to ensure the correct allocation of resources, with a general plan of:

Telephony:	Requirements	Infrastructure	Reporting		
Quality:		Requirements	Infrastructure	Reporting	
Complaints:			Requirements	Infrastructure	Reporting

The key challenge for this plan is likely to be the time taken for signoff by the operation after the reports have been created. Once the two contractors have left, it will be much more difficult to make large amendments to the infrastructure and processes.
In order to improve the signoff process, collaborative workshops with key operational stakeholders are likely to help here.

Scenario 2: Transforming an executive reporting and insight team

Reporting type	Regulatory	Permanent FTE	4
Data tool	MS access	Contractor FTE	0
Reporting tool	Excel and Power BI	Contractor tenure	N/A

Remit: Provide weekly and monthly packs on regulatory metrics with commentary and insight.

Initial period	

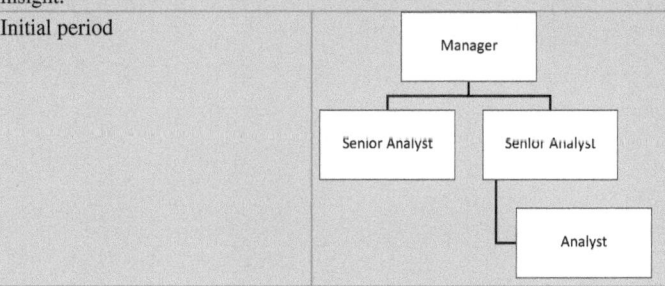

Scenario 2: Transforming an executive reporting and insight team

Long-term goal

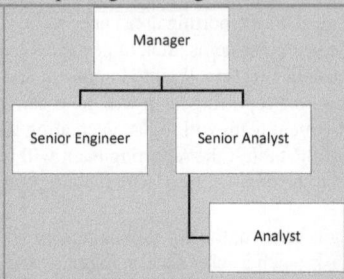

Technical strategy: You have been asked to transform a regulatory reporting team, and upskill them to use power BI to improve the team's reporting capability.

The team is struggling with workload due to the large amount of time regular reporting takes and additional pressures from ad-hoc requests.

Power BI will deliver a powerful reporting capability, but it will not solve the underlying issue of this team. The data strategy should come first. The goal should be for BAU reporting to be as seamless as possible, and as close to automated as we can manage with the tools at our disposal.

The initial team structure does not have enough focus on data and development, so we will either need to upskill one of our colleagues, or look to bring a senior engineer in.

It is imperative that all changes you make to this team are carefully considered, work towards your final strategy and do not disrupt the ongoing regulatory reporting the team undertakes.

Upskilling a current team member will be difficult with the team's workload, so if this is the route to be taken, the manager should look to get involved in the regular reporting to free up development time.

Open and honest conversations with stakeholders and senior management should also be held to curb the number of ad-hoc requests, with the end potential of much more timely and more insightful analysis.

Scenario 3: Rationalising several teams into one group analytics function

Reporting type	Group	Permanent FTE	18
Data tool	SQL server	Contractor FTE	0
Reporting tool	Power BI	Contractor tenure	N/A

Remit: Combine three existing data analytics teams into one.

Scenario 3: Rationalising several teams into one group analytics function

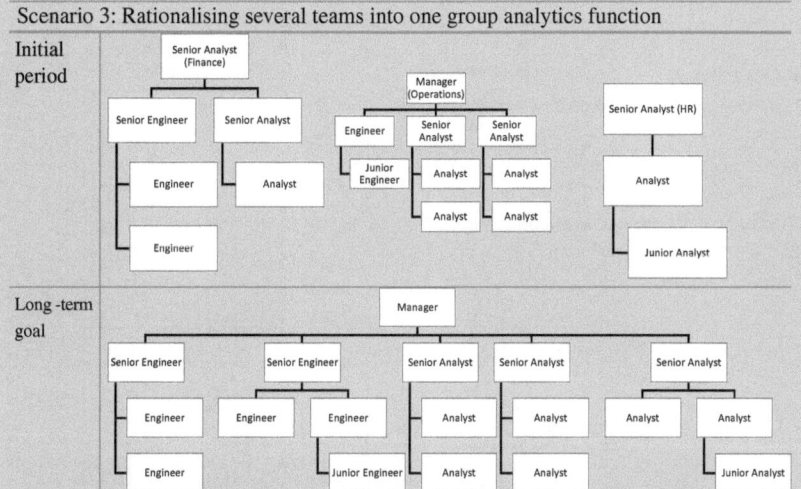

Technical strategy: In this scenario, three data analytics teams are being joined together to form a centralised group data analytics department.

Power BI is used across all three teams; however, only the operational team uses SQL server, with the other two using excel as their data source.

Misaligned reporting, and an inability to create a group view of analytics have driven this company to centralise their data analytics teams.

The finance and HR team data sources will need bringing into SQL server to provide the benefits of being able to combine the three functions together, and this is going to take time.

More engineers are going to be required, so we need to think about transitioning some of our colleagues from analytics roles to engineering. This switch can be a popular one and is usually not hard to find colleagues who will be actively looking for this change. The analysts from the HR and finance teams will need to learn SQL, and this is not an easy task. Whilst a visualisation tool may take weeks to learn, a new coding language can take months, even a year if this is their first coding language.

Maintaining the BAU reporting throughout this integration will be key, along with not over-selling the capabilities of the new infrastructure. There is a risk of too many requirements coming into the team, through which a behemoth of a task is created and never fully realised.

The reporting focus once the data ingestions are complete should be on creating holistic reports that give an overall picture of each function, allowing for the BAU reporting to be decommissioned, freeing up analysts time to continue the development of the reporting.

The biggest hurdle in this project will be communication by the manager of the team, in providing an overall strategy and achievable goals for each member of the team.

Scenario 4: Organisational downsizing for an IT reporting team.

Reporting type	Service availability	Permanent FTE	12
Data tool	PostgreSQL server	Contractor FTE	3
Reporting tool	Tableau	Contractor tenure	3 months

Remit: Provide service availability reporting and insight for the organisation's three key operations

Initial 3 months

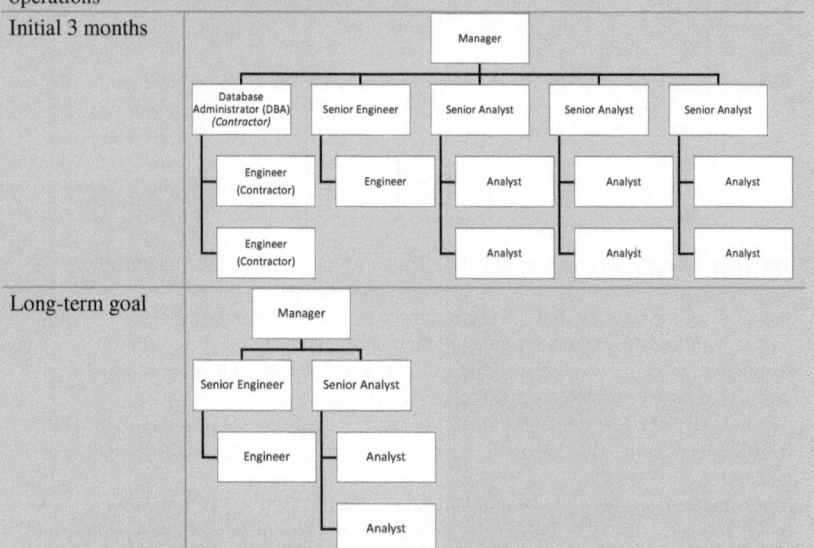

Long-term goal

Technical strategy: In this scenario, three contractors have been brought in to facilitate the downsizing of a reporting team from 10FTE to 6FTE.

The reporting team already uses tableau, which is used to create reporting from MS access and excel data.

Data quality and a great deal of time spent processing data manually are likely to have been the catalyst for the need to transform the team, by delivering a reliable data infrastructure.

Time is of the essence for this project, and it is imperative that the contractors brought in to facilitate the new infrastructure alongside the permanent engineers are not burdened with improving any of the existing reports or BAU requests and solely focus on a new infrastructure, with the reporting analysts spending significant time supporting these contractors; providing requirements, testing and documenting the infrastructure as it is built.

"Agile Project Management" techniques *(discussed later in this book)* will be invaluable, as the largest challenge will be ensuring the new infrastructure is completely tested before the contractors tenure finishes.

Whilst building the infrastructure, a focus on future amendments must be considered by the engineers. Look-up lists, conversion tables, and large "case/if coding statements" must all be made easy to maintain.

By heavily involving the report analysts in testing and documentation, the knowledge of the infrastructure the contractors and permanent engineers are creating can be passed on. This will also ensure the whole team is fully invested in the new infrastructure, and as enthusiastic about its potential as possible.

These scenarios are unlikely to fit your use-case, but hopefully the themes within each one will be similar to the ones you will encounter.

Knowing where you want the team to get to, what the possibilities for transformation are, and what structure of team is required, is extremely important at an early stage. The initial questions you will get from your management will be; what can be achieved and in what timescales. It can be very hard to change the expectations of your management and key stakeholders further down the line.

3.5   When the Structure Doesn't Work

The structure of a team is not likely to be perfect.

Requirements change over time, the weighting between data and analytics, between report development, insight and stakeholder management will constantly change.

However, it is important to realise when the structure of a team has become so out-of-line with its requirements that it starts to become dysfunctional.

The easiest way to explain why this happens is to give examples.

3.5.1   Top Heavy Management

There are many situations in which a reporting team will be made up of senior colleagues. An IT Service Delivery MI team is a common example. Each senior analyst within this team will be responsible for the reporting of service metrics to a different department, and as they engage with senior leaders, must be senior enough to have the stakeholder management skills for the role.

These teams will often have very few engineers, and little technical knowledge within the senior analysts, which have been chosen for their stakeholder management skills.

With insufficient skillsets to develop and maintain reporting, reporting can often go horribly wrong, and because of the senior nature of the team and stakeholders.

3.5.2   Lack of Senior Leadership

The inverse of the previous example, this reporting team will be made up of entry level analysts and/or engineers.

The reporting consistency and accuracy will often be high, but without enough senior leaders to interface with senior stakeholders, the team finds itself too reactive to the demands of stakeholders, too many ad-hoc requests and reporting changes, and no long-term strategy to deal with these issues.

These teams tend to flounder in high-workloads and have a high-turnover of staff.

3.5.3   Lack of Engineers

This is the most common of these examples. A team of reporting analysts who have great skill in BAU reporting and insight, but lack the skills to develop reporting and transform data.

Such teams create overly manual and time-consuming processes that over time become unwieldy and massively complex.

The most obvious signs of such a team are spreadsheets with dozens of data and calculation tabs.

These teams will have a very high workload as BAU reporting takes over their schedules, leaving no time for development of their reporting. Ad-hoc reporting is difficult due to the complexity of the reporting, and reporting inaccuracies, errors, and manual mistakes become commonplace.

3.5.4   Engineer Heavy

Teams largely made up of engineers with few analysts are most commonly found within IT reporting departments and are often responsible for the provision of reporting self-service tools rather than reporting and insight.

Without the stakeholder management skills, and a lack of engagement with the areas they support, these teams will tend to become overly bureaucratic, and engagement from the business becomes slow and preventative.

Due to this, the reporting tools provided become quickly out of date with changes in the business, and end users of these tools end up copy and parting metrics from them into their own reporting, creating localised reporting teams. The infamous "cottage-industry" is often created as we discussed previously in Sect. 2.1.

3.6   The Right Question

Inevitably, there will be issues in your new team, either in what needs accomplishing, or what is already in place.

To find a solution to this you will need to first seek answers from your managers, team, and stakeholders.

The answers you are seeking are not just to what is going wrong, but what ideas your colleagues have to make things work. Additionally, what they see as "good".

The answers you get back should form part of your strategy and should not be ignored, but they also might not be right. Often, a team that has been struggling to cope with workloads for a long period, will fail to see a way out of the issues they have.

It is important that we don't just focus on what is going wrong, where the problems lie and how to fix them, as these questions focus on immediate change without considering a long-term strategy.

The right question to your team is always: "Where do you want the team to be?"

The right question to your stakeholders is always: "Where do you want the reporting to be?"

Such questions that explore the "art of the possible" allow you to gauge the potential of your team, gain insight of what they can see which is often not visible to their management, allow your experts to reveal their insight, and also help inspire your colleagues to think of the long-term goals of a team. We want to give our stakeholders the freedom to talk about what their challenges are, what is happening in the business, so we can assess how we could help them with data and reporting solutions. In asking such open questions we avoid the restrictions they might think we have. This is discussed in detail in Sect 7.1.

3.7 Meetings After Meetings After Meetings

Meetings can be useful, but often they are not.

No doubt if you look in your calendar for the week ahead, you will find that most of the meetings have colleagues attending that will not contribute or benefit.

Meetings not only take time away from colleagues to get work done, but they break up the day, meaning larger pieces of work need to be completed across several periods. This break in concentration and focus increases the overall time taken to complete a task, as colleagues revisit what has already been done, and recap the requirements.

Ensure your business culture does not support this. Collaboration and stakeholder engagement are great. Meetings for the sake of meetings need to be avoided.

In different roles, the percentage of time spent in meetings will vary. Usually, we see this increase as roles become more senior and less technical (Fig. 3.1).

In the table above, analysis has been carried out to identify the amount of time being spent in meetings within data and analytics departments. These are actual averages taken in 2021, and the low levels of free time for colleagues to carry out productive work are alarming.

Not only do you need regular time to concentrate on your work, but a productive meeting should have time for preparation before, and reflection afterwards. If this is not needed, then perhaps the purpose and usefulness of the meeting should be revisited in the first place.

> I happen to believe that in every day, you need some quiet time to think. Where you are not being bombarded by external forces. In some cases, you are not doing e-mail. You are not watching television. You are not doing anything but enabling yourself to concentrate on whatever it is that you might be anticipating or what you are planning to do. That's vital.

Fig. 3.1 Banking industry analysis of meetings and roles [2]

Role	Time spent in meetings %
Junior Engineer	8%
Senior Engineer	41%
DBA	23%
Business Performance Analyst	49%
Reporting Analyst	35%
Senior Reporting Analyst	45%
Manager	63%
Senior Manager	64%
Head of Function	74%

—Bob Iger, Disney CEO [3]

Blocking out time for thought is a tool that is being implemented more and more by senior leaders, and proving a very effective way to improve the way we work.

3.8   Chapter Summary

1. Draw out the team structure you need now, and when your team is matured.
2. Consider how the team will develop, what new skills you will need, and how you will transition roles.
3. Look for signs that a team structure isn't working.
4. Protect your team from too many meetings and too much bureaucracy.
5. Prepare for leavers and absence.

References

1. *Undergraduate 2022 Software Engineering BSc/MSc.* Glasgow University (2021) https://www.gla.ac.uk/undergraduate/degrees/softwareengineering/
2. *Banking Industry Analysis of Meetings and Roles.* John Mackay, (2022)
3. *Lectures at Masterclass* Bob Iger, Disney CEO. (2019) https://www.masterclass.com/

Chapter 4
Data Sources

4.1 The Importance of Data

Data is more important than the reporting itself, both the accuracy of it and the understanding of it. The consequences of using data for reporting without a comprehensive understanding and awareness of it can be severe.

Understanding is required to know that you are using the data in the right way. Just because a field of data appears to contain what you want, are you sure it includes everything you need?

Awareness of what the data does and how it is made, informs you why things are changing and helps to identify what is happening. Is a new business trend emerging? Is this an issue in the data?

A great data strategy will mean reports can be built that are/have:

1. Far quicker
2. More accurate
3. Fewer iterations in development
4. Faster report refreshes
5. Better audit
6. Lower risk
7. More responsive
8. More dynamic
9. More flexible
10. More interactive

Knowledge of your own data is also key. Not just for your engineers, but for your reporting analysts, the team management and even senior management who are making decisions impact the team.

Take the time to ensure that everyone understands how the data works and how it is used.

J. Mackay, *From Data to Insights*, https://doi.org/10.1007/978-981-96-3545-0_4

It is very common for engineers to take a project or piece of work, and deliver the data to the analysts without an explanation of what everything is. By ensuring the knowledge of how the data works is shared, you will be able to improve the reporting of the whole team.

It is equally as common for analysts to request data from engineers, without providing the background of what the data is, or what it is doing. This can have major impacts if the engineer does not know what can be expected to change within the data, or where the focus of the analysis will be.

Data is organic. It takes on the personality and characteristics of the team that have created it and worked with it, and of the framework that has been put in place by the management.

The way tables have been built and linked, and the code written, varies enormously from team to team and from engineer to engineer. The interaction between team members and the characteristics of how the teams work is defined by the framework that has been established by the team's management.

It is immediately obvious to an experienced data practitioner when they look at the data structures of a poorly performing team in comparison to a well-performing team. The attitudes of the team, the way they implement code, build reports, and interact with stakeholders are similarly easy to distinguish between good and poor management.

Here is a list of some of the most common reporting issues:

1. Too many ad-hoc reports
2. Too much rework
3. Too tight deadlines
4. Too much to do
5. Reporting takes too long
6. Reports taking too long to build
7. Report errors
8. Poor reputation
9. Reports look bad
10. Unhappy stakeholders

At first glance, all of these may appear to be related to how your team's reporting is built and the report analysts.

However, all are likely to be directly related to a poor data infrastructure.

Let's take a look at how our data strategy can mitigate each one of these issues.

4.1.1 Too Many Ad-Hoc Reports

Most ad-hoc reporting can be avoided. By ensuring data is held at a granular enough level to answer potential ad-hoc requests, we can add functionality into our reports that allow the report-users to access this data when they need. *(This is discussed in detail later in this book).*

4.1.2   Too Much Rework

When the data is held in a format designed for reporting, very few calculations and formulas are required in reports. This completely changes the process of building or amending a report. Instead of rewriting formulas, rebuilding report sections and ensuring consistency between different parts of a report, changes, and rework can be made in a few minutes.

4.1.3   Too Tight Deadlines

When the data infrastructure has been built to answer not only the immediate questions, but also potential future questions, the work required in developing new reporting can be done up-front in the data long before new requirements ever come in.

This is much easier than it initially sounds. By ensuring our data captures a type of reporting at any level it could be asked for, we can create an infrastructure that can answer future questions easily.

Not only will this help the team to hit tight deadlines, but it can widen the scope of what is possible and allow a team to innovate and offer more than the stakeholders anticipate you can supply. Your team will love you when they have the capacity to work proactively, rather than reactively.

4.1.4   Too Much to Do

Too much reporting is a sign of a large number of very specific reports. Each report having its own requirements and its own calculations and logic.

When new report development is requested, the data infrastructure should be prepared first. Not just to provide the immediate scope of the reporting requirements, but capable of a much wider potential.

This will allow for fewer reports to answer more questions.

With fewer reports and datasets to manage, the amount of work the team is required to carry out reduces.

4.1.5   Reporting Takes Too Long

A report should take seconds to refresh not minutes, it should have no manual "copy and pasting" or data manipulation, there should be no need to "copy formulas down", "add in new tabs", or any other such manual steps.

By moving all of your data manipulation into centralised and dedicated processes, these issues can be avoided.

Most of the time, slow manual processes are employed by a reporting team, because they do not have the knowledge of what is possible with the data they have.

4.1.6   Reports Taking Too Long to Build

When developing a new report, the build of the report itself should take no more than 20% of the total amount of time spent to build the data and report.

An optimal data infrastructure means that the 80% of data preparation can be done in advance. The development time of a report then becomes hours, rather than days or weeks. (Though the review time of a report is highly dependant on the experience and knowledge of your analysts.).

4.1.7   Report Errors

Reports almost always error because of formulas, data manipulation, inconsistency, and lack of foresight.

The formulas and data manipulations often appear essential and faultless before they break.

By moving these processes to the data layer of your reporting, these issues can be avoided. We are able to centrally amend calculations and metrics so fewer changes are required. We can future proof reports by removing elements that can cause issues, or creating exception processes to mitigate for new values. Data can be reused for future reports, and so we only need to test and validate it once.

4.1.8   Poor Reputation

The reputation of a reporting team is built upon its reporting quality, accuracy, timeliness, consistency, and ability to adapt with the business.

All of these can be vastly improved by implementing a great data infrastructure.

4.1.9   Reports Look Bad

How a report looks is usually a function of how the data looks.

Whilst it is possible to manipulate data within a report using formulas and calculations, this is difficult and leads to large, slow, and difficult to maintain reporting.

By taking control of the data and ensuring it is always in the right format and level of granularity for the reporting, more functionality can be garnered from a report. So, reports can be built that look better, are more responsive and interactive.

4.1.10   Unhappy Stakeholders

Any one of the aforementioned issues will impact upon the relationship your team has with its stakeholders.

Your stakeholders, however, will not know the root cause of your reporting team's issues. Reporting, or colleagues will invariably be blamed, when the issue stemmed from the data infrastructure.

4.2   Data Imports

The way data is brought in to a team and stored will impact every part of your data and analytics processes.

How and where you store your data is a decision that will impact many aspects of your reporting. Once you have committed to a path, it can be very difficult to unpick and amend later.

Most commonly data will either be ingested to your data infrastructure through an automated data feed or a manual extract.

When there is an option, the automated option should always be picked for reliability, speed and to reduce potential errors.

Where a manual extract is necessary, there are still options of how to do this, and the least manual option should always be picked, which leaves the least amount of room for human error.

Data Feed Options Ranked Best to Worst
- A server-to-server (or API) connection where your team "pulls" the data is the best option.
- In addition to be able to be fully automated, this allows retries of the data import when the expected number of records are not received, or when there are network issues.
- A server-to-server (or API) connection where the supplying team "pushes" the data.
- This allows for a fully automated import of data, however should there be an issue, you will need to contact the source data team to get them to retry the data push.
- An automated extract from a system. This is common where external access is not permitted to a system database. This is similar to the "server-to-server push" above, however has more potential for issues to arise due to the additional step required in placing the data to a mutually accessible location.

- A manually saved dataset which is automatically imported. Most commonly this data will be received by e-mail *(but could also be an extract from a source system)*, which is then saved by an analyst to a dedicated folder. The data will then automatically be picked up and pulled into your server/data storage.
- This relies on the source data file never changing, and the analyst always remembering to save the file.
- A manually extracted dataset pasted into a table. Most commonly a tool like MS access will be used to allow a colleague to copy data into a table.
- Preferably, this data should be pasted into an empty table, which is then automatically added to the full dataset, rather than allowing the colleague to paste straight to the full dataset. This avoids potential problems in overwriting data.
- This type of process is often used by teams who expect to have to manually updated values in a table later. However, usually this is through lack of understanding around how this could be done more reliably and safely, by utilising audited tables, described earlier in this chapter.
- Manual data pasted straight into a report.
- This option carries all the risks of any manual process, but also means the data will only be accessible to this report. This in turn will make it difficult to use the data elsewhere, makes the reports larger than required, and invariably means manual addition of calculations are required.
- Finally, we have options of data manipulation, which whilst commonly used by many teams, do not even bear consideration.
- Copying a dataset from one tab of a report to another. Often used in exec reporting to ensure a static history is saved and changes not possible. This can be an understandable approach, though reusing previous data and tracking trends over time becomes very difficult. These could have been easily stored in a audit/history table.
- Transforming data manually using "vlookups" or calculations, then pasting to another location. Extremely popular in teams that work with data such as finance, HR, planning and ESG teams, mistakes are very frequent. These teams need to work more closely with the teams that supply the source data and more importantly, data analytics teams who can provide better solutions.
- Directly entering data without copying and pasting where this would have been possible. This is dangerous, and will go wrong quickly. Estimates for human error should be taken into consideration any time there is manual input and validation ensured, if it cannot be avoided.

4.3 Data Source Types

For most companies, there will be a wide variety of data source types used, each one chosen for a specific purpose. The architects of each system have a range of data structures and technologies that can be implemented, and the data and analytics team will need to work with these.

Much of the work in extracting these various data types are carried out by integration tools, which are developing rapidly.

Be careful when choosing the tools you want to use to accomplish these imports. As companies move to cloud applications, which are discussed later in this book, processing carried out in the cloud architecture can carry a cost. Data transformation and processing are often relatively more expensive than the import itself. Carrying out transformation of data during the import can carry an even higher cost.

You may see the terms of ETL and ELT. These are "Extract, Transform, and Load" (ETL) and "Extract, Load and Transform" (ELT). The difference being in the order of processes. In ETL, we transform the data as it is moved, in ELT we transform it after we have imported it.

For ETL, there may be a higher cost associated with the import; however, we may be able to create a smaller data size, and save on storage costs.

For ELT, we replicate the data imported onto our server, and then create transformations afterwards. The import will be cheaper, but requires a higher storage capacity. Usually storage costs are far cheaper than processing costs, but this will be dependent on your specific scenario.

4.4 Big Data, Non-structured, and NoSQL

Big Data Refers to very large collections of data. These data sets are typically too large to be processed traditionally and are usually held in non-structured or NoSQL data stores.

Non-structured Data Includes files such as photos, emails, audio, or sensor data. We can still use integration tools to extract the data from these files, though we will need to convert this data to a format we can report with.

SQL and NoSQL If SQL is "Structured Query Language", then NoSQL just refers to "Not Only Structured Query Language".

What we really mean is that SQL data is tabular, whilst noSQL uses a different structure that is not so easy to process for reporting. There are a few types of NoSQL datastores, the most common for business being JSON file storage.

A JSON file provides a key and value to represent elements of the data (Fig. 4.1). Multiple values can easily be added to each key.

We can report directly from a noSQL data store using some visualisation tools, or we can transform this data into a tabular structure (Fig. 4.2).

Transactional Data Think of this data as many entries, each one describing a thing that has happened. This is more likely to be referring to a normalised view. As the name infers, transactions such as from a cash machine or sales are entered in one after the other.

```
{
  "id": 1,
  "name": "Carl Sagan",
  "contact": {
    "email": "carl.sagan@cosmos.com",
    "phone": "+19876543210"
  },
  "expertise": ["astrophysics", "planetary science", "science communication"],
  "metadata": {
    "birthYear": 1934,
    "deathYear": 1996
  },
  "publishedWorks": [
    {
      "title": "Cosmos",
      "type": "Book",
      "year": 1980
    },
    {
      "title": "Pale Blue Dot",
      "type": "Book",
      "year": 1994
    }
  ]
}
```

Fig. 4.1 Example of JSON code

astronomer_id	astronomer_name	email	phone	birthYear	deathYear	expertise_area	published_title	published_type	published_year
1	Carl Sagan	carl.sagan@cosmos.com	19876543210	1934	1996	astrophysics	Cosmos	Book	1980
1	Carl Sagan	carl.sagan@cosmos.com	19876543210	1934	1996	planetary science	Pale Blue Dot	Book	1994
1	Carl Sagan	carl.sagan@cosmos.com	19876543210	1934	1996	science communication	NULL	NULL	NULL

Fig. 4.2 Example of JSON code transformed into a SQL table

Relational Data   This describes to the relationship of data within a table rather than the relationship between tables. This is more likely to be referring to a denormalised structure. Calculations are usually already done on this data. This will often have volumes of data rather than individual entries for each one.

4.5   Historic Data

Your data strategy needs to consider how to handle changes in data and historic data.

This could be a phone number of a customer being updated; the outcome of a case being re-evaluated or the value of an account changing. For each one, the data will need to be updated to reflect this change.

However, when data changes historically, you may never be able to recreate previous reporting. Whilst this may not matter now, it probably will in the future. At some point, you will be asked to explain how metrics in a previous report came to be. Because the data has now changed since this report was created, it becomes very difficult to show how the report was derived.

There are three main ways to deal with this:

1. Saving the data in your reports, and saving historic copies of each report. I would not advise this. It will mean your data stops being centralised, and any queries upon previous reporting need to be carried out in isolated datasets, rather than from your core data store. This will make analysis difficult and make future work very time consuming.
2. Saving snapshot data. This is most commonly used for end of week/month reporting in which reporting is created once a period has ended.

   Each period, a snapshot of the entire dataset is created, saving every piece of data required in a date-stamped table.

   In SQL, SAS, MS access, etc. this may look like tables named:

   Finance_Metrics_2021_01
   Finance_Metrics_2021_02
   Finance_Metrics_2021_03

   The benefit of this is that once created, the tables are set in stone and you can be certain no changes are made. This tends to be used for regulatory reporting with which requirements can never change for historical data.
3. Creating "Audited" tables. These are tables that contain both the previous version of a record and a new record, with variables or dates to identify the most up to date record.

   This is by far the best option for most scenarios and will enable both historical reporting and current reporting from the same table with only small adjustments to your report logic.

Audited Tables
(Also known as history tables, historisation, versioning, change/event/activity log or tracking tables.)

In the example below, the record number 1001 has been updated with a new value, changing from 102.34 to 102.32.

Current reporting would only use records which do not have a Record_Valid_To date; however, we can show how this record looked in May 2021 by only looking at records where the current date is between the Record_Valid_From date and Record_Valid_To date (Fig. 4.3).

Record Number	Revision	Metric	Record_Valid_From	Record_Valid_To
Record 1001	1	102.34	2021/04/05	2021/06/07
Record 1001	2	102.32	2021/06/08	

Fig. 4.3 Example of audited table entries

4.6   Qualitative and Free-Form Data

Qualitative data is, by its very nature, difficult to report on.

Most commonly, qualitative data will be stored "free-form" text fields, in which there is little control of what can be typed, though it can also be found in non-structured formats as discussed in Sect 4.4.

To use qualitative data in reporting, we would expect the full text of each record to be used individually to give a complete context to a piece of data, or we would expect to perform analysis on this text, to search for certain words or word-patterns.

Searching within fields is slow and cumbersome. It is always quicker to perform these processes within a server or dedicated system/tool, than in an end report.

Free-form data usually contains errors. We cannot and should not expect anyone to enter in data with 100% reliability. The way we design data searches and checks should accommodate for mis-keying and misspelling.

In some cases, we can design systems to mitigate these risks, such as by ensuring a telephony number is of the right length and format, and only contains numbers. In most cases, we will not have control over this, and so should try to highlight data errors through exception reports, warnings, and alerts. *This will be discussed in more detail later in the book.*

4.7   Manual and Unreliable Data

Manual, unstructured and unreliable data is the hardest type of data to deal with.

When designing a process to capture this data, or bring it in to your reporting infrastructure, you will need to consider not just how it is imported or created, but how it is checked and then double checked.

It is very common for a reporting team to use external data. When this is the case, we have little or no control of their data quality and consistency.

Where possible, a template should be provided to the team sending in the data. This will encourage the external team to provide the data in a consistent way, and no to change/add/remove columns, change data types, or add entirely new data or tabs.

Nonetheless, this data is often essential for the business, and so we must find ways to bring in the data reliably.

There are many ways to do this, which will be specific to your teams' structure, tools, and capabilities, so we will not detail the methods. However, as a manager, it is important to ensure there is adequate rigour around checking the data when it comes into your team.

> **Example: Data Checking**
> Examples of data checking:
>
> 1. "Indexes" can be put on your tables, so that unexpected values in the data cause errors which are flagged.
> 2. Logic can be added to reports to look for new values, and then highlight these in your reports.

System	What not to do	What to do
Excel	=IF(Country="England","England","Scotland")	=IF(Country ="England","England",IF(Country ="Scotland","Scotland","Unexpected Entry"))

SQL	CASE
	  WHEN Country = 'England' Then 'England'
	  ELSE 'Scotland'
	END AS Country
		CASE
		  WHEN Country = 'England' Then 'England'
		  WHEN Country = 'Scotland' Then 'Scotland'
		  ELSE 'Unexpected Entry'
		END AS Country

Power BI (DAX)	IF('Country'[Country] = "England","England","Scotland")	= SWITCH([Country], "England", "England", "Scotland", "Scotland", "Unexpected Entry")

Fig. 4.4 Examples of logic in various languages

3. Ensure that any logic within your infrastructure does not assume what an unclassified entry is (These will be discussed in more detail later in the Sect. 5.1) (Fig. 4.4).
4. Create exception reports that notify your team, or the team sending in the data when new values come in, fields are unpopulated, or errors arise in your processing of the data.
   (These will be discussed in more detail later in the Sect. 8.3.1).

4.8   Protecting the Data

When designing the processes and tools whereby users will access data and analytics, a huge focus must be paid to which users have access to what, the confidentiality of the data, and the rules and regulations in place in your organisation.

Confidential customer data, colleagues scores and performance, sensitive business models, and overviews so comprehensive they would pose a risk if they were leaked out of the company are all examples of access to data and analytics that needs to be controlled.

If your organisation has a risk partner/department, this is the opportune time to get on a call and discuss the options with them. There will usually be limitations in place to what types of data can be sent via different means, can be saved to folders, on intranet sites/tools such as SharePoint, Teams, and how access to these needs to be controlled.

Password-protected files are usually a bad idea. Passwords still need sending out to access files, which are often easy to guess, and can additionally often be removed using widely available tools.

Files saved to folders with limited user access can work, but care must be taken to ensure the access lists for these folders is maintained.

Emailing reports out to only the required users is a common method for distribution of reporting, but contains many potential security issues, such as emails going to users who store their personal email files on a shared drive. There are also likely to be policies in place to stop confidential information being emailed.

Specialist encryption software offers a solution for many of these issues, though does come at a cost and usually a few hoops to jump through to get users access to send and receive files.

So far, we have focused on sending out data and reports which could be manually or through automated processes. However, we must also consider users with direct access to our datasets/databases and what they can see.

For most databases, views (or sometimes queries) can be created that allow users access to see a filtered, calculated, or limited view of the data in the tables. User access rules can then be set up to only allow certain users access to certain views. This allows very granular control over who can access what.

Thinking back to the reports that we send out, if these contain the code which accesses the database, then we must ensure any end users cannot manipulate this code to access data we don't want them to on the database.

It is possible to password protect the code in many tools, though this isn't always all that secure. Another way to secure the code could be to use database functions *such as a scheduler ETL in SQL* which allow the code of the report to be saved in the database, which is then referenced in the report.

Different views can be created of the same dataset that allows users to see different fields. This technique may be employed if we want to show a non-confidential and a confidential view of the same data. This way we can easily allocate view access to the correct users.

Views can be used even more effectively by combining different views, or by changing which data/fields can be seen based on who is refreshing the report.

By doing this, in data visualisation tools or reports, a non-confidential view can be presented, then when locally refreshed by a user with access to the confidential data, this confidential data presented.

It should be remembered that any solution for disseminating confidential data in your business should be checked with any relevant IT, risk, or governance teams.

Chapter 5
Data Processing

5.1 Combining Data

Should your team need to join data from multiple sources, link multiple tables from the same source, or use lookup lists against your tables *(This includes lengthy IF, IN, CASE, Option or Switch statements)*. Then you will need to consider how this is done.

Potential values in a dataset can and do change over time. New products, categories, outcomes, and the renaming of these are common examples.

To cater for these, processes should be designed from the outset to allow for changes to these datasets that facilitate this. Reference (or mapping) tables are the best way to achieve this.

Below is a simple example of how this can work, using a sales table, then reference tables so we can translate the values in the main table into understandable outputs (Fig. 5.1).

These reference tables can then be controlled through tools, or standard processes, so changes can easily be made. This can even be extended to the end user if they are more likely to hold the required information.

Sales Fact Table			Product Reference Table			Outcome Reference Table	
Product	**Outcome**		**Product**	**Product_Description**		**Outcome**	**Outcome_Description**
Box	Sld		Box	Standard Box		Sld	Sold
Lg Bottle	Rtn		Bottle	Large Bottle without filter		Rtn	Returned
Box	Rtn		Clip	Bicycle bottle clip		Rtn web	Returned via Website
Clip	Sld						
Box	Rtn web						

Fig. 5.1 Examples of fact and reference tables

A further benefit of this is that when a new value appears in the Sales Table, because we don't have a corresponding value in the reference table, we can easily see it is something we have not dealt with before. At this point, we can create automated communications or flags in reports to alert our engineers, or whoever is responsible for updating these reference tables with the new values.

In businesses with a multitude of data sources all being combined together, these reference tables become the backbone of ensuring data consistency and allow us to combine data from vastly different datasets together.

A user ID or product ID in one system may vary to another, so a reference table can help to join these together. Sometimes the scale of the reference tables can seem disproportionately large, but the benefits usually outweigh the cost when we are able to leverage the combining of datasets and the added functionality and insight this can give us.

A final note on this is that we should always plan for the future. Change to our infrastructure can take a long time to implement. If we wait for a request to be raised to add in new reference tables, change the way tables join or are stored, then the subsequent changes will take much longer than if they were integrated from the start. Alternatively, if they can be proactively identified as being useful before they are essential, we can save the business a huge amount of time in being able to quickly turn around requests.

5.2   Functional Fact Tables

When we have brought in all the relevant data sources to our data warehouse/server, combined linked data together and incorporated reference data to translate values into understandable business outputs, then we next need to look at creating functional fact tables.

These are tables that bring together multiple tables that all relate to the same thing, so that we can create a centralised table from which all of our reporting and insight on this element can use.

An example of this might be combining several tables with sales data in, all from different systems. These would be combined into one table, with any relevant calculations and transformation carried out. This would then be the only table referenced in the team's reporting and insight regarding sales.

There are several benefits for this.

1. Should a new table or system be introduced, this can then be included in an existing fact table, and so no changes to the rest of the infrastructure or reporting needs to be made.
2. Any calculations, transformations, or reference lookups only need a change being implemented in one place.
3. Testing for reporting is made much simpler.
4. Confidence that all reporting matches and is aligned is much higher.

5. Reporting analysts and data scientists need only understand these fact tables, instead of learning the structures and processes behind in each individual system.
6. Engineers will spend much less time trying to work out the impacts of a change, as the downstream impacts of a change can be only from these fact tables.

For some systems, there will be different types of fact tables for the same systems.

We may need to have a customer-level, case-level, action-level, payment-level, etc. This is absolutely fine, though it should always be considered whether any of these could be combined.

5.3 Data Principles

5.3.1 Consistency

Consistency saves time, makes our framework and reporting easier to develop and understand.

When every table on a server uses the same rules, whether these are naming rules, structure or processes, it becomes easier for the engineers to work on and for analysts to report from.

When every report uses the same template, formats, styles, methods, and approach, it also becomes easier for our analysts to work on and for our stakeholders to understand.

In both situations, by improving consistency, we are able to reduce the time it takes to apply what we know about one element to another.

Should an engineer or analyst who has only ever worked with one type of data, support another colleague working on a type of data they have not seen before, consistency means this is so much easier and better collaboration is facilitated.

5.3.2 Back to the Drawing Board

In 1914–1915, Albert Einstein was developing a theory on the geometry of space-time and its relation to matter. This was one of the last stages of completing his monumental theory of general relativity.

Einstein worked on these equations intensely, and after a year of trying to develop them, he realised that the track he had been working on had a fundamental issue (Fig. 5.2).

The issue was, for mathematicians, a simple one. For the lay-person, unfortunately this is not the case. If the description that "these equations were not covariant, and so could not always be applied in all frames of reference", means something to you, then great. If not, then we just need to know that Einstein had spotted an error in his work.

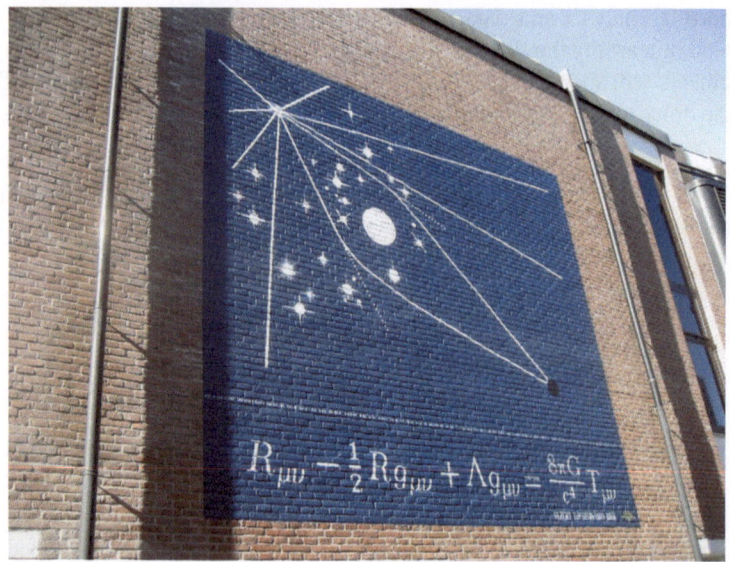

Fig. 5.2 Einstein's field equation in Leiden, Netherlands (https://commons.wikimedia.org/wiki/File:EinsteinLeiden4.jpg)

Instead of continuing down this route, or hiding what he had done, he owned up to the error, and took his equations back to the drawing board.

Starting again, he was able to rework through the process of creating his equations, this time with an understanding of what had gone wrong before. He may well have been able to continue with his previous path, and eventually turn it into the correct one, but he foresaw that it would have taken much longer and would have been inefficient [1].

Knowing when we need to start again and go back to the drawing board is a lesson that is much more difficult to learn in data and analytics.

Frequently we will find reports and code that has "evolved" over time, becoming more complex, more lengthy, less understandable, harder to test, and more prone to failure.

The problem is that pieces of "spaghetti code" or reporting with several steps become so complex, and so an addition to this process is much easier than starting again from scratch.

Time constraints are most often the major concern for the team, and this is where a manager must step-in and create the time for the team to redesign the entire piece of work.

This will save time in the long-run, as changes to the new process will be simpler and easier to test. It will also reduce the risk of unforeseen errors being in the code/report or arising at a later date.

Additionally, this will also engender the right attitude in the team of "doing things the right way" and not taking shortcuts.

Going back to the drawing board also applies to the framework of the team as well as the individual components.

The sooner we start to challenge and approach major changes, the better. If these are left as-is, then any development and work that is carried out in the mean-time may have to be redone.

There may be scenarios where the changes that need to be implemented are so large, you will want to segment them, or align them to other changes. Remember that these should be coordinated into your overall strategy.

5.4 Complex Data

The complexity of the data you will need to report on is not always self-evident.

The more data sources you need to link together, the more complex the infra-structure will be. But this does not mean the underlying data will be more complex.

As a data and analytics manager, when required to pull in an additional data source for reporting, the normal consideration is to ask:

1. What will this data be used for
2. Who will receive it
3. Is it replacing something already in existence
4. Are there defined requirements for the reporting
5. How will the stakeholders receive and use this reporting

Whilst all these are very important questions, it leaves out the most important aspects that will define how long it will take your team to decipher and be able to use this new data source in reporting. These are:

5.4.1 What Structure Is the Data In?

Normalisation

The data is stored in many tables, each one doing a very specific task, from storing a range of values for one field, to providing a link between these fields. There may be hundreds or thousands of these tables. This type of structure is very fast to save data into, but also very complex to work with.

This type of structure is typical for applications and is usually how your data will start out.

In some situations, you may want to keep this structure for reporting, usually if you have a front-end tool such as Tableau, Business Objects, Power BI, etc.

Denormalisation

The data is stored in fewer tables, with attributes to the data stored side by side. The table will have a field in for every value you will need, and will look very much like a set of data you will see in Excel. Usually, this data will have been transformed already from a normalised view, in preparation for reporting.

This type of structure is faster to report from as joins between tables are not required, and also easier to understand, but is much slower to write data into.

It is important to think of normalisation and denormalisation not as two separate things, but as two approaches to data structure. Data can, and is most often, partially normalised, so a blend of normalisation and denormalisation are utilised.

> **Example: Data Structures—What Does This Look Like?**
> **Normalised Structure (Fig. 5.3)**
>   This is not a completely normalised structure, but has the level of normalisation you are likely to meet in reporting.
>   **Denormalised Structure (Fig. 5.4)**

5.4.2   Further Complexity: Data Processing

In many cases, especially for normalised or transactional data will require processing after you have received the data.

A simple example of this would the average duration of calls answered during the day. This cannot be calculated throughout the day, as you need to know the total number of calls and the total duration. Then divide one by the other to get the average call duration.

A more complex example would be working out how many customers entered a store, using a sensor on the door. This would use the calculation of how many times the sensor was tripped divided by two. Assuming everyone that goes in must come out. The complexity increases with more doors. This also does not give a great

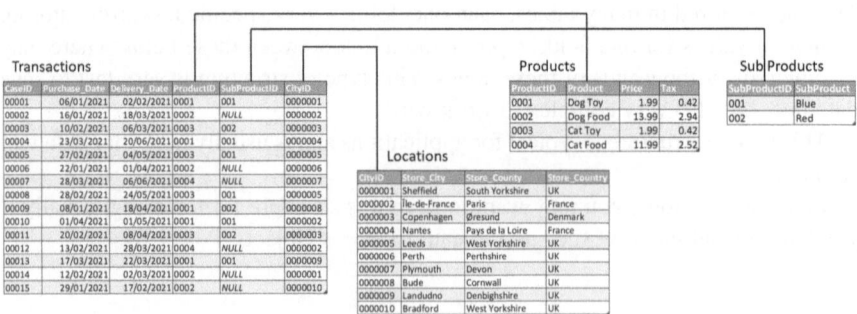

Fig. 5.3 Example of normalised structure

CaseID	Purchase_Date	Delivery_Date	Product	Sub_Product	Store_Country	Store_County	Store_City	Price	Tax
00001	06/01/2021	02/02/2021	Dog Toy	Blue	UK	South Yorkshire	Sheffield	1.99	0.42
00002	16/01/2021	18/03/2021	Dog Food	NULL	France	Paris	Île-de-France	13.99	2.94
00003	10/02/2021	06/03/2021	Cat Toy	Red	Denmark	Øresund	Copenhagen	1.99	0.42
00004	23/03/2021	20/06/2021	Dog Toy	Blue	France	Pays de la Loire	Nantes	1.99	0.42
00005	27/02/2021	04/05/2021	Cat Toy	Blue	UK	West Yorkshire	Leeds	1.99	0.42
00006	22/01/2021	01/04/2021	Dog Food	NULL	UK	Perthshire	Perth	13.99	2.94
00007	28/03/2021	06/06/2021	Cat Food	NULL	UK	Devon	Plymouth	11.99	2.52
00008	28/02/2021	24/05/2021	Cat Toy	Blue	UK	West Yorkshire	Leeds	1.99	0.42
00009	08/01/2021	18/04/2021	Dog Toy	Red	UK	Cornwall	Bude	1.99	0.42
00010	01/04/2021	01/05/2021	Dog Toy	Blue	France	Paris	Île-de-France	1.99	0.42
00011	20/02/2021	08/04/2021	Cat Toy	Red	Denmark	Øresund	Copenhagen	1.99	0.42
00012	13/02/2021	28/03/2021	Cat Food	NULL	France	Paris	Île-de-France	11.99	2.52
00013	17/03/2021	22/03/2021	Dog Toy	Blue	UK	Denbighshire	Landudno	1.99	0.42
00014	12/02/2021	02/03/2021	Dog Food	NULL	UK	South Yorkshire	Sheffield	13.99	2.94
00015	29/01/2021	17/02/2021	Dog Food	NULL	UK	West Yorkshire	Bradford	13.99	2.94

Fig. 5.4 Example of denormalised structure

picture as two customers could walk in together, so the length of time the sensor is tripped for may be used, or two sensors one after the other to gauge direction may be employed. An algorithm would then be employed to calculate the number of customers based on the data, as this calculation would be too complex and time consuming to carry out on a dataset spanning a large period.

5.4.3 The Impact to Your Strategy

The important part of what has just been described *(and you definitely don't need to fully understand this—that is the job of your engineers)* is that the complexity of data is not in how many rows, or even fields of data you have, but how this is structured.

If your team is bringing in a feed from a new data source, one that is denormalised (or relational) will be relatively easy to bring in, and may only take a few hours or days to implement.

However, one that is normalised (transactional) will take significantly longer. If overnight data processing is also required, this could be months of work.

Example: Scenarios

To help you understand the timeframes, here are some real-world examples of the length of time I have seen in an experienced and highly qualified team:

1. An in-house quality control system where the data is provided in a denormalised view, with excellent documentation being provided.

   This took an engineer just 1 day to bring the data into a SQL server, create tables to house the data with a view sitting on top to calculate the outcomes of each case.

2. A workflow management system with a normalised structure, utilising under 10 tables. No documentation, but an SME (Subject Matter Expert) from the originating team to explain how the tables are joined and what calculations will be required.

   This took an engineer a week to implement, though was delayed a month at the start to allow the SME to have enough capacity to spend time with our engineer. Testing of the end product was also delayed by a week as this required time from the SME again.

3. New dispensing machines was introduced to stores, which were entirely transactional and fully normalised. Downtime, faults, and transactions for the machines were stored in an events log. One entry per fault start, fault end, or transaction. Multiple faults could overlap each other. Additionally, no documentation was supplied, and no SME provided to assist.

   This took a team of two engineers and an analyst 6 months working solely on this task to implement.

5.5   Tables and Views

In Sect. 5.3, we discussed consistency. This is incredibly important to our tables and views.

5.5.1   Tables

A data table is just like a table in a book. It has structured columns and rows, and a header (name) for each column (Fig. 5.5).

A table is actually stored somewhere and takes up space. This can be a table in SQL, Oracle, Access, Excel, or even its own file like a CSV.

Each system will have its own rules about how a table is created, and what can be in each field. Whilst every system is different, there are a few basic rules that should be followed.

1. Only use alphanumeric characters in column headers.
2. Never use spaces or special characters in column headers.
3. Avoid using special characters in data where possible.

A table is an independent data object.

Once we have created a table, we can add, change or remove the data in it.

Fig. 5.5 Example of a table

Sale_Date	Sale_Type	Sales
2021-10-29	Grass Seed	4
2021-10-30	Corn Seed	3
2021-10-30	Corn Seed	5

Fig. 5.6 Example of a view

Sale_Date	Sales
2021-10-30	8

5.5.2 Views

A view is a virtual object that summarises, transforms, or filters one or more tables (Fig. 5.6).

The example above is using the previous example of a table. In this view, we have limited the data to only be the 30th October, and wanted to see all sales for this day.

A view doesn't hold the data itself, so it does not take up any space (only the space to describe itself).

In Excel, a pivot table is a view, rather than a table as it does not hold data itself. Having said this, it is possible to save the data connection within a power pivot table.

5.5.3 Which One Is Best?

Usually, we receive data in a structure that we need to transform or summarise to be more useful.

The data we receive is put into a table, or new data is appended to an existing table. Then from this we start to transform the data to make it more useful for us. This may involve combining tables together into something completely different. When we do this, we have the choice to save this as a new table or a view.

We query data from a view and a table in the same way. In most coding languages, you may not even realise whether it is a view or a table.

A table will be quicker to query than a view, as the view needs to recalculate everything from the original table, whilst the table has its new data stored. However, the view does not take up any space, whereas the new table is taking up space. So, there will be a trade-off between performance and storage space. There is no best, it is situation dependent.

There are additional considerations. We can more easily control which users are able to view what with a view in most systems, or to change what data we are displaying depending on the date, what time it is run, what system it is run on or who by.

Because of these reasons, it is good practice to ensure reports query views rather than tables directly, and end users given access to the data have access to views rather than tables (Fig. 5.7), however these views should not have filters rather than calculations and transformations within them, and vies tables which have been precalculated, as this combines both speed and security/ease of reporting changes.

When we are transforming data from the original table provided, into a final summary, it is likely there will be several steps to this process.

In the example above, there is just one step between the tables and the view the end user will see. In practice, the steps between the source data and the end view can easily increase over time.

The more steps we have, the more complexity, and therefore the more things that can go wrong. Equally more tables and views will have to be developed if there are changes to the base data.

On the other hand, if the queries to transform the data become too complex and unwieldy, then this in turn can cause issues.

So, there is a trade-off between having fewer steps with more significant changes between each one, and having many steps with smaller changes between each one.

There are a few things we need to be wary of here.

1. Too many steps with complex changes in between.
2. New steps added to the process that should have been included in the existing ones.
3. Different routes of data which describe the same thing.

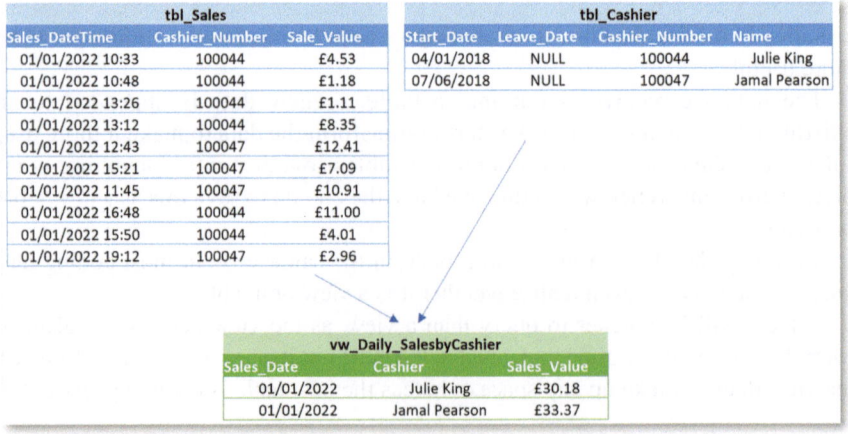

Fig. 5.7 Example of tables being transformed into a view

To show these in action, below is an example of the same data being used in two different process flows (Figs. 5.8 and 5.9).

On the left, we see a process that has evolved over time, as new reports have been requested, so new views and tables tagged onto the process flow. Very quickly the complexity builds up.

On the right we see how this could have been either redesigned or strategically envisioned.

It should be easy to imagine how much work would be involved in making changes to the example on the left in comparison to the right, and how much harder it will be to ensure changes made are reflected in every view and report.

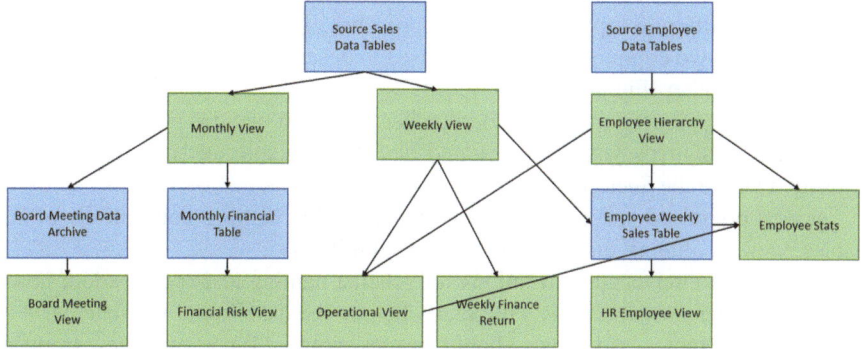

Fig. 5.8 Example of an evolved process flow

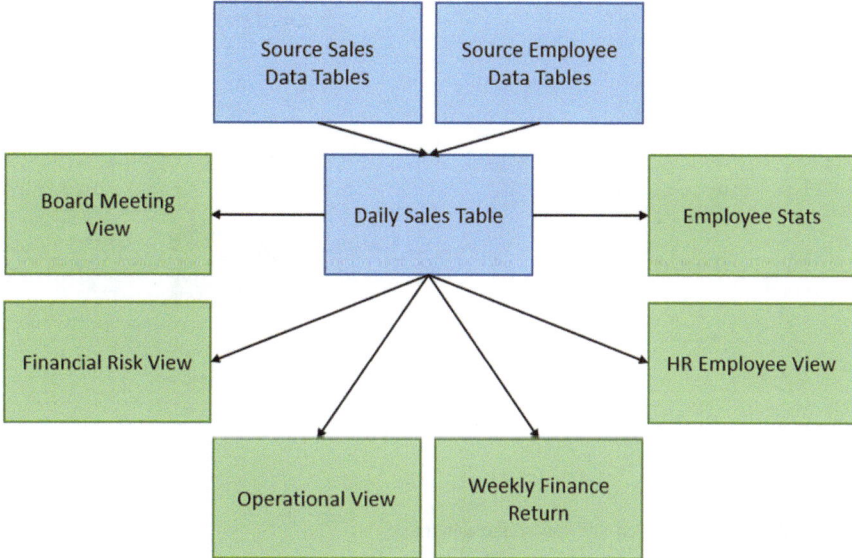

Fig. 5.9 Example of a strategically designed process flow

In reality, the process flow on the left is often not understood by the team. Rarely is the flow of data from one table or view to another documented outside of the database, so changes to one piece of the puzzle have unintended or even unnoticed consequences elsewhere.

5.5.4   Schemas and Organisation

The process flows we have been discussing are termed "schemas". A schema also includes other database objects that may be used on the database such as indexes and functions.

There are different types of schema approaches. The star schema or snowflake schema being two common ones that are used to describe how the tables and views relate to each other (Fig. 5.10).

Which one you need to aim for, or whether you use a blend is normally dictated by what data sources you are using and how the schema needs to work. These closely relate to the Sect. 5.4.

A well-organised schema will have standards for naming conventions of its tables, views, columns, and any other objects it utilises.

There are no universal conventions for schema naming and organisation; however, setting our own standards will greatly help in the usability of the schema.

Names for tables and views should be descriptive. Types of tables grouped together to make it obvious what they are doing.

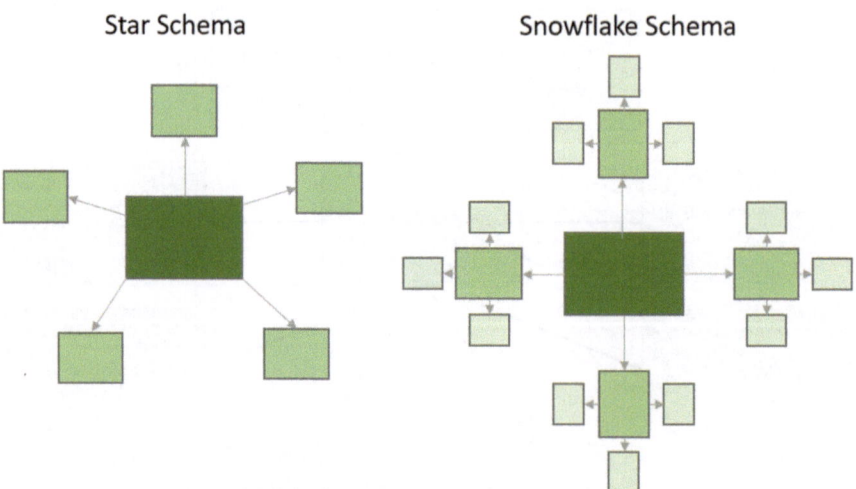

Fig. 5.10 Examples of star and snowflake schemas

When databases grow larger, it might be an idea to split out very different data into different databases on the same server, such as data that will support an End User Computing (EUC) tool, should be split from an unrelated system's data.

There is an argument that tables should not be prefixed "tbl_" and views should not be prefixed "vw_" as these datatypes are defined in the information schema (the metadata of a database). However, by using these prefixes, we can make it easier for review of the code at a later date to understand what has been used. Though we don't need this, it can save a great deal of time in very large and complex databases.

To understand how this organisation looks when interacting with the server through a tool like Microsoft SQL Server Management Studio (SSMS), there is an example below: (Fig. 5.11).

In the example above, the components of the server are the following:

1. Server Instance
2. Database
3. Schema
4. Table

Every time we reference data within the server, we always need to include the schema and table names. The database can be set at the start of the query (if only one is used) and omitted later, and the server instance is rarely used (unless you have linked servers).

As the database grows with more and more tables and views, it becomes essential that the schema and tables are named logically and consistently. This will save a good deal of time in searching for the correct tables and later administrative operations which requite bulk updates to multiple tables.

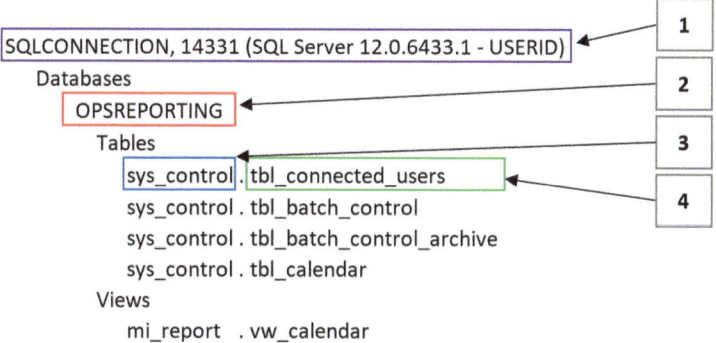

Fig. 5.11 Example of SQL schema naming

Reference

1. *Einstein's Mistakes*. Steven Weinberg, University of Texas (2005) https://physicstoday.scitation.org/doi/10.1063/1.2155755

Chapter 6
Other Data Considerations

6.1 The Cloud

Moving your databases and services to "the cloud" has become has become the standard for many companies recently. AWS, Microsoft, IBM, Google, and Oracle are some of the large providers of this technology.

The cloud can be a scary term for those that have not encountered it before.

However, the cloud is really just a different way of storing data. When we store our data on servers that are physically in our business, we call this "on—premises". When we move the service and their data to a virtual framework in which the servers can be located anywhere, we call this "on the cloud".

The reason we would want to use a virtual service is that the servers are essentially replicated on many or multiple instances and so, are more difficult to have service issues. Our infrastructure needs to connect to these virtual servers usually over the internet. With massive developments in encryption, the safety is of these connections is usually better than of our own internal infrastructure.

Many different systems and programs can move to the cloud. Office 365 is an example of this, which is a cloud supported service. Your files and data are stored virtually yet can be accessed very easily on your PC. Should there be a problem with your PC, then your files are all backed-up on the cloud and your laptop can be rebuilt to exactly the same situation you left it before.

This creates a very risk averse framework, however does have its problems. Maintenance of the servers held virtually may need to be carried out by the provider of that cloud service. However good this service may be, it can never be as good as an on-site dedicated engineer or DBA in your team.

When several cloud services are integrated, there can also be expected to be lengthy engagement periods for the set-up of the services, and more difficulties encountered in getting them to work in the first place. The initial expense of the systems is sometimes much higher and will almost always carry a higher ongoing cost.

J. Mackay, *From Data to Insights*, https://doi.org/10.1007/978-981-96-3545-0_6

For large organisations, the benefits of moving various services and data to the cloud often far outweigh maintaining their own servers, managing upgrades, and having a physical presence for their upkeep. For medium and small organisations, it will be situation dependent.

6.2   Enterprise, Off-the-Shelf, and In-House Products

There are three types of software we need to be aware of, enterprise, off-the-shelf, and in-house built.

6.2.1   Enterprise

An enterprise system or ES *(sometimes called an enterprise management system or EMS)* is a system built by another company that is tailored specifically to your company.

Often used interchangeably, an enterprise resource planning or ERP is similar, but not quite the same as an enterprise system. Instead, an ERP would be a modular part of an ES, namely the automation of business processes, managing inventory and planning. An ES contains an ERP, but with additional functionality that might include analysis, suggest new markets and control competitors.

An ERP is typically used by medium or large businesses, whilst an ES would only be used by large businesses.

The implementation of an enterprise product will have an initial cost of setup, then an ongoing cost of maintenance. It is important if you are involved in such a project that the ongoing maintenance includes the chance to be able to raise additional changes and requests as your business changes and develops. An enterprise product that is inflexible and has too high a cost-barrier to make changes to is one that will rapidly become irrelevant to the business and require replacement.

6.2.2   Off-the-Shelf

An off-the-shelf product is a software application that is commercially available to an organisation and provided as a standard product.

Applications such as Excel, Tableau, Business Objects, and Power BI are all off-the-shelf products.

Off-the-shelf products will be far cheaper than enterprise products, much easier to find training for and easier to find online support for on internet forums.

6.2.3   In-House

An in-house solution is one built within your own organisation.

These are less common than enterprise or off-the-shelf products, as the organisation will need to have its own software development team to develop it.

The major concern in dealing with such solutions will be the ongoing maintenance of them. Often, a project to create such a product will end when the software goes live and a short bedding-in period. Following this, changes become very difficult, as the expertise to build this software may have moved on to other projects.

Similar to this, but on a much smaller scale is an EUC.

An end user-computing system or EUC is an in-house built system that has been developed using an application such as Microsoft Access that facilitates development through a graphical interface to avoid the need for coding the application from scratch.

EUCs tend to be common, but risky. They can be created easily by engineers, analysts, or any other colleague as they have a very low technical entry criterion. Whilst this is a great way of enabling users to build their own systems, it is much less likely that the users building these products will have the expertise and technical skills to build in the checks and balances and controls that we would expect to see in an application.

6.3   Data Science

There is no universally agreed definition of what data Science is, and the definitions you find may vary quite dramatically. For the purposes of this book, **data science is the discipline of turning data into actionable insights.**

The distinction of when data processing and analysis is undertaken as data science rather than data development/analysis is most easily understood by whether the data being worked with is structured data or unstructured data. Data engineers and analysts typically work with structured or known data, whereas data scientists work with unstructured or unknown data to derive forecasting, predictions, and what-ifs.

Data science roles may require a different set of coding languages to be understood than an engineer or analyst, though they can often work with the same tools. Tools such as Hadoop, SAS, and Python are three major languages used in data science, though they can all be used for data analysis as well.

Which tool is used in data science is not actually all that important, what is important is that the data scientists have been able to add value in a way that ensures their analysis can be verified, is reproducible and is actionable.

Whether this is a quick and easy piece of analysis in excel, or this is lengthy and complex using the most advanced data science tools does not matter. What matters is that the business can have faith in what has been concluded and can achieve value from this piece of work.

6.4   Artificial Intelligence and Machine Learning

These terms are likely to conjure up images of science fiction *(possibly dystopian)* futures.

Fortunately, at the time of writing this book, we *(humanity)* are still a long way off being able to create true human like general purpose artificial intelligence. If you are not a practitioner of one of these disciplines, then it is important you understand what they are in terms of data and analytics and their limitations.

6.4.1   Algorithms

To understand artificial intelligence and machine learning, we need to start at the base of computer programming, algorithms. An algorithm is an automated instruction. It is typically one of the first things you will learn when using formulas in excel, or a new coding language.

To give an example, we will start by considering a simple line of logic.

If the animal says woof, then it's a dog.

In a computer language, the algorithm might be written as one of these:

```
SQL:    CASE WHEN animal_noise = 'Woof' THEN 'Dog' END AS
animal_type
Excel:    =IF(animal_noise="Woof","dog")
```

This example is not great. Do other animals say woof? Do some dogs howl or yap?

In this simple algorithm, we can easily improve it and make this much more complex why adding other clauses, such as the animal must be furry, or to add if the animal says "miaow" then it is a cat.

6.4.2   Machine Learning (ML)

Machine learning is the use of algorithms that learn from data, tag values, and draw analysis based on patterns.

To give an example of machine learning, forecasting the number of phone calls we will receive is a good place to start.

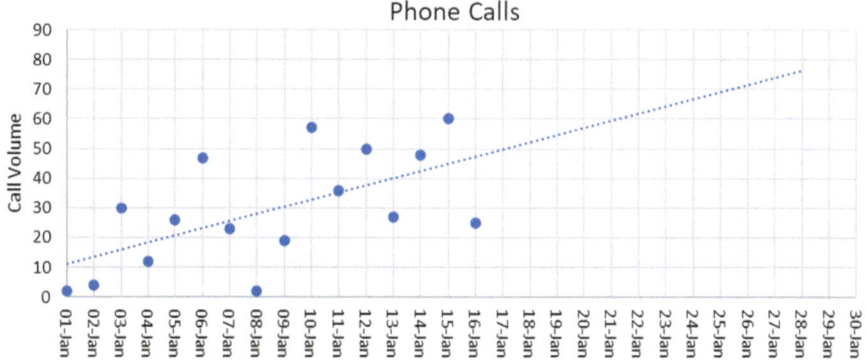

Fig. 6.1 Example of a telephony prediction

We will first need to know the number of calls we have had over a certain period. From this, we can then use an equation to work out the average trajectory of the calls, and so have a guide by which we can predict future calls (Fig. 6.1).

This is actually terrible. We haven't thought about a whole host of variables that impact this, such as what day of the week calls are on, what demand is driving the calls, impacts on the callers and seasonality. The period over which we have looked is also far too short.

In practice, using machine learning could have thousands of different inputs. From this, we then create a model to fit a sample size of our known values. This is called training. This is then tested on a larger set of data to validate if it works.

The example we have given is of **supervised learning**. There are other approaches including **unsupervised learning** and **reinforced learning**.

For a simplistic view of this, these two other types of machine learning would work as follows in the example above: Within **unsupervised learning** we would not label that the call volume was, or any other input. We allow the machine learning to create the equation with less guidance from the programmer. Within **reinforced learning**, we would use a trial-and-error system, in which the model is amended each time a successful or unsuccessful outcome is achieved. This provides a feedback loop, which is most akin to how a human naturally learns.

6.4.3   Machine Learning in Practice

Machine learning can be incredibly complex, and it can relatively simple. This depends on whether we are using existing libraries and models, or developing our own.

For most business uses of machine learning, we utilise libraries that have been created for us. This is similar to whether we use off-the-shelf software, enterprise software, or in-house built software (Sect. 6.2).

Example: Image Recognition Using Python

Python is a data science language commonly used in machine learning, with a large range of libraries we can utilise to create models, which can analyse and predict data for us.

Below is an example, using the libraries from Scikit-Learn in which our model learns from a library of 1797 handwritten numbers, what each number should look like [1].

In the first block of code, we set up our environment and specify which libraries we want to use. In the second block of code, we train our model on 20% of the available images, then create a prediction on a random sample of 12 numbers. The final block is just creating a visualisation of this so we can assess if it has worked or not (Fig. 6.2).

Our model has taken 12 images of handwritten numbers and predicted what it thinks each number is. In this example it has done well.

If we were to decrease the training dataset it has to work with, we would find that these predictions decrease in accuracy (Fig. 6.3).

We can actually quantify the accuracy of the predictions by joining this back to the data to see how our accuracy has changed. In the first example, we used 360 samples with a 97% accuracy, whilst the bottom one uses 36 examples and has only a 67% accuracy.

```
import matplotlib.pyplot as plt
from sklearn import datasets, svm, metrics
from sklearn.model_selection import train_test_split
from sklearn.metrics import accuracy_score
```

```
digits = datasets.load_digits()
n_samples = len(digits.images)
data = digits.images.reshape((n_samples, -1))
clf = svm.SVC(gamma=0.001)
X_train, X_test, y_train, y_test = train_test_split(data, digits.target, train_size=0.2)
clf.fit(X_train, y_train)
predicted = clf.predict(X_test)
```

```
_, axes = plt.subplots(nrows=1, ncols=12, figsize=(10, 3))
for ax, image, prediction in zip(axes, X_test, predicted):
    ax.set_axis_off()
    image = image.reshape(8, 8)
    ax.imshow(image, cmap=plt.cm.gray_r, interpolation="bilinear")
    ax.set_title(f"Pred: {prediction}")
```

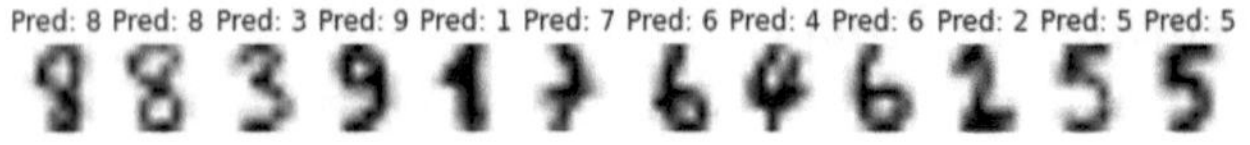

Fig. 6.2 Image recognition in Python

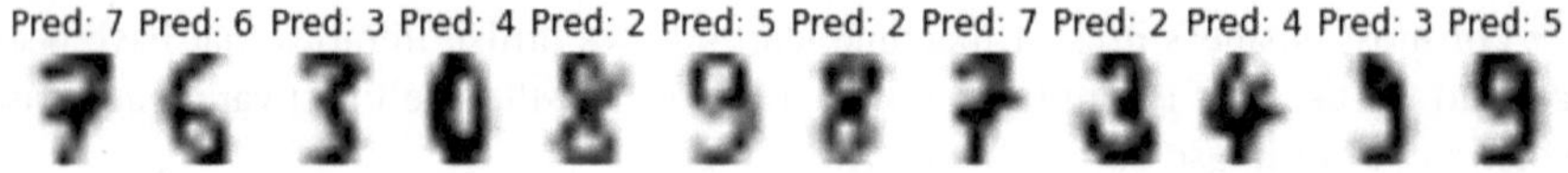

Fig. 6.3 Image predictions from Python

6.4.4 Artificial Intelligence (AI)

Artificial intelligence is the use of pre-tagged data models and prompts to generate outputs such as text, images, and decisions by predicting the next value in a sequence, in order to mimic human decisions.

Since late 2022 when ChatGPT was launched, the definition of AI changed with the improved developments coming through. I have no doubt within a few more years, the definition will need to be revised as the capabilities of AI grow.

Artificial intelligence uses large datasets, called models. Within these, each input (word/image, etc.) is tagged with known elements. The AI then predicts the next word or output in that sequence based on what is has seen so far. This is very similar to ML. The difference being that AI attempts to create decisions like a human.

The outputs of ML would give the most likely next word in a sequence. The outputs of AI would give the most human-like output in a sequence.

Within analysis, most of the time we are dealing with AI projects in a business environment, we are really just talking about algorithms and machine learning. We would expect to use AI much less frequently.

An example of business AI that you might encounter is a chatbot. This is a tool that engages with customers, which we can use to answer customer questions.

We could have a simple chatbot that uses rules, much like in our algorithm example. This would not be AI. When we have a chatbot that attempts to mimic human behaviour, looking at what is being said and how it is said, what keywords are being used in relation to others to continue a conversation we would have an AI chatbot.

In this example, we could use natural language programming (NLP) to assess the language being used by a customer, derive the sentiment. This may sound complicated, and it can be, but with the right programming language, a lot of the work can be done for us (Fig. 6.4).

Within the workings of the NLP module "textblob" used in the example above, analysis of which words are used, what type of words and their proximity to other words is undertaken. This generates a value identifying the negative or positive opinion (polarity) of the customer between 1(negative) and 1(positive), with this example being −0.6, a moderately negative opinion.

This can then be used in combination with other elements such as the subjectivity and objectivity of the language used to construct a conversation that is much more human-like, than if we just searched for certain words using a simple algorithm.

Other examples of AI being used in business would be quality checking text, diagnosing conditions or faults, predictive maintenance, fraud detection, and personalised text.

```
from textblob import TextBlob
sentence = 'I am really unhappy with the way I was treated in your store'
print(TextBlob(sentence).polarity)

Result: -0.6
```

Fig. 6.4 Simple use of NLP in Python showing a negative customer opinion

AI is not conscious, sentient and is not human intelligence. It is also currently very fallible, and highly likely to make mistakes. As AI improves, it becomes harder and harder to spot the mistakes it makes, which are sometimes termed hallucinations. Sometimes it will seem to make up facts, as the training data does not help it form a logically correct conclusion. If you do embed AI into your workflow, especially generative AI, then you need to ensure there is a feedback loop in place to check the outputs it creates.

6.5   Automation

There are many tools available for automation. Some are likely to be built into your infrastructure already as standard. How automation is implemented with your chosen automation tool varies greatly from tool to tool, and as progress in these applications is rapid, so descriptions about individual ones here will not be of much use.

Automation should be viewed as the way to free your team to work on worthwhile activities. Your engineers should not have to spend time cleansing or loading regular data imports. Your analysts should not have to spend time refreshing or even distributing reports.

All of these tasks can be automated. A well-designed infrastructure can automatically pull in data, process it, refresh reports, and distribute them. A great infrastructure can also perform many other checks on the data and free up your team to work proactively on the goals of your team, leaving the regular churn of reporting behind.

To choose the right automation tool for your team, we must first assess how this automation is going to work. This will be a question for your senior engineers to decide on and implement, as they will know what approaches will work for your business, and which tools they have the most experience with. However, there may be other tools with a cost attributed that will be a better option. This is discussed in the Sect. 2.4; however, it is incredibly important that we reiterate how essential it is to hold conversations about what technologies we want to use with our experts and teams.

An automation tool will need to be installed or housed somewhere. Wherever this is, we must consider the impact of that system or service also failing.

A system/process running on a computer: then what would happen if that computer has an issue? Perhaps it has been switched off by cleaners, has rebooted following an update, or has inexplicably just stopped working. This doesn't preclude you from using a computer-based application. Ways around this would be to use multiple computers, even at multiple locations. This could have the benefit of sharing the load between computers, so processes could run concurrently.

A system/process running on a server, then this will be less likely to have issues, but your engineers, or IT department will still need to have options available for server issues.

A system/process running on a cloud server, this will be even more reliable, though with the same issues as a server.

Finally, a third-party service for automation. In this case, the management of service issues may be addressed by the provider, or one of the three previous routes may be used.

6.5.1 Automation and FTE

Once automation is setup, it is very important that the team's management understand that this is the start of your drive to being an excellent team, not the end.

Maintenance of an infrastructure, no matter how automated, maintenance of reporting, building new capabilities, and reporting are extremely time consuming.

Many managers that go through an automation journey do not realise quite how labour intensive both manual data manipulation and reporting is, but also how labour intensive maintaining a data and analytics infrastructure is.

The difference is that once you have automated the infrastructure, then the reliability, quality, and functionality of your team's work can be far superior, and the ability for your team to work proactively rather than reactively can be unharnessed.

6.6 Risk

In many organisations, risk is left to dedicated teams to manage. Whilst these teams perform a vital role, it is a mistake not to thoroughly consider risk in your own team's every day activities.

The consideration of risk of aspects of your team allows you to control and reflect on all the elements of a team being discussed in this book.

The way a manager assesses and reviews risk can become the main control mechanism of a team, and this will be a great asset.

Here we are going to look at types of data risks and how we can mitigate them.

6.6.1 Dependencies

Each system, person or place you receive data from is a dependency. This might be a receipt of data from a source system, or it could be a new target provided by another team.

Wherever the source, these are all dependencies that you need inputs from, and without them you will have gaps in your data and/or reporting.

When your data sources have issues, either through late running or incorrect data, you need to hold them accountable. This needs to be done as soon as practical. Let them know, and give them a chance to resolve it.

Automation can provide the tools we need to improve upon this, as discussed in the Sect. 6.5. There are a number of ways we can utilise this to spot issues and mitigate risk.

Completeness, Accuracy and Timeliness (CAT) standards are often used to spot issues in the data we receive

1. *Do we have enough data? (Completeness)* When data is supplied to your team it will usually either be an update of the whole data set or just the previous day/period (known as "deltas"). We can set criteria for how much of a change in volume of data is concerning. Perhaps a 5% or 10% difference limit, after which we send alerts out. Just remember to think about how variances might occur in the number of records received by day of the week, or after a bank holiday.
2. *Is the data right? (Accuracy)* We can check to see if it has the right date range in it, whether any products or categories of data are missing, or even is something new has come in.
3. *Has the data arrived yet? (Timeliness)* Testing if source data has arrived by a certain time is a very useful and straightforward task. From this, we can either alert our own engineers to contact the responsible team, alert the responsible team directly or alert our stakeholders or end users there is an issue.

6.6.2   Poor Data Quality

Any system that uses data input by a human is liable to fail. Even a certified courtroom stenographer will only achieve a 98% accuracy rate, so we must plan for erroneous values in our data.

For an operational reporting team, there will most likely be quality teams who sample cases are worked by colleagues. However, this will usually only be a small sample size when the colleague has become competent enough to reach certain criteria.

Later in the book in the Sect. 8.3, we will discuss how we can work with the business to improve this. Sometimes, this is not possible. If your team receives data from a regulator, or third party for which you have no ability to influence them, then this is often not possible.

For now, we need to think about the impact this will have to our data infrastructure.

Most systems will have a combination of system driven fields, dates, drop down options, and freehand fields in which anything up to a certain length can be typed. In more rigorous systems, there will be checks on what has been entered to see if it conforms to what is expected in that field. Unfortunately, this is often not the case.

For any field or data point that can impact our reporting, we need to think about what would happen in our infrastructure if something erroneous or unexpected is entered. Here are a few examples to start the ball rolling.

- Has a date been left blank? If so, should we assume another populated date field should replace this one?

- Is a reference number in the correct format or length? Do we have limitations in our code that would exclude this entry, or do we need to include it, but put it in a new category?
- Does a colleague ID exist in our hierarchy, or reference number exist in another system? If so, then is it more important to have all the data, or only data that matches?
- Has a new value been seen in a field such as brand, product, or country? How will this be reported in our data?

Such assessments need undertaking for every field that we use in our infrastructure. Without this, our data and analytics will surely be wrong.

To mitigate this risk as much as possible, we can add "primary or foreign keys" to fields in our data that could prevent duplicate values, or we could add error handling or alerts to manage potential issues.

6.6.3 Lack of Skills and Cover

If we don't have the skills, experience or knowledge in our team to carry out a required task, then we will have a risk.

Some work can be done to mitigate this risk by ensuring that our colleagues are cross-skilled across various activities, which is discussed in detail in the Sect. 3.3.

When planning which technologies to utilise in our infrastructure, we must also think about the skills in the team, and whether we would expect future replacements to be able to support these. Occasionally your team will be handed a process created by another team. Perhaps this is a SAS process, whilst your team works with SQL, or an excel workbook with large amounts of VBA in.

When this happens, it is important that we spend the time to rewrite these in technologies that our team can support. Whilst the particular process may run perfectly well now, should there be an issue, or changes required in the future, the team ability to handle this work may not exist.

It is always better to proactively develop a solution, than to wait until that change is forced upon you. Murphy's law of "everything that can go wrong, will go wrong" definitely applies to data analytics teams, with the additional criteria of "at the worst possible time".

6.6.4 Lack of Business and External Awareness

A risk that rarely graces the ARIAD (Assumptions, Risks, Issues and Dependencies) logs of project managers is the impact of things changing outside of your team, either within the business area you support, the teams that supply your data or in the world outside of your work.

When the Financial Crisis of 2008 or the Corona Virus pandemic of 2019 hit, there was little most data analytics teams could do to predict these happening, but an awareness of what was going on differentiated teams that would struggle and teams that would cope.

By thinking about what is happening outside of your team, changes can be proactively made to improve the data you hold and the reporting you do.

Any financial reporting team at the Financial Crisis could have foreseen an increase in mortgage and debt defaulting, customers needing additional support or collapse in asset values.

Any operational reporting team at the start of the Corona Virus pandemic could have foreseen the need of colleagues to work from home, and so additional functionality in reporting to support this was obviously going to help, or again financial impacts to customers and other businesses.

As a team, you will need an external awareness of when your systems will reach end-of-life and stop being supported, when updates and upgrades will be coming in, or ever when new systems are being developed that would improve the operation of your team.

6.6.5   Storing Code

Generally speaking, the closer we can have calculations to our base tables, the better.

In terms of risk, it is more likely for functions and calculations in reports to go wrong, than when these are included in tables or views on the server.

Some calculations need to be included in our end reports, for instance, when the numerator or denominator of a calculation can change due to functionality in the report. To put it simply, if the report has slicers, buttons, dropdowns, or options to change what can be viewed, then any averages, percentages, or summing calculations need to be in the report.

For automated reports, the code that refreshes the report is often held within the report. Perhaps you have also enabled the end users to refresh a report when they want. The potential risk with this, is that the report they have been given is run at a later date; a week or year later? In this time, your team might have changed the logic required for this report.

A log of what reporting is held outside of your team might work for this, or you could store the code on your server. This latter approach is more involved, but by putting the report code into a view, package or script on the server, only a reference to the code needs to be included in the report, and so future changes can be made in the knowledge that any report refreshes will reflect these changes.

6.7   Ethics

Data ethics are ever more important in the age of AI and the increasing integration of data through each company. We must consider what data we collect and why we are collecting it, then how we store it and finally what we do with it and how we process it.

6.7.1   Data Retention

When data is ingested from the source systems of the business into our reporting servers, our imports might delete all of our existing data and replace it with data from the source system. In this case, the duration of data held in the source system will match our own. Therefore, we will need to find out from the source system owners what data retention policies they have, and if these will be applicable to the data analytics team. Alternatively, we may take just the latest data from the source systems. In this case, we need to ensure our engineers have built processes to remove old data from our server depending on the data retention policies of the company.

6.7.2   Data Types

When we bring in data to our reporting servers, we do not always need the full detail. We can take a summary for some data sources, for instance, we might not want transactional data at a transaction level, instead we might want to capture volumes for the hour or day. We also might not want to bring every field into our server.

Depending on the regions in which your company operates, different laws applying to different types of data. The laws governing German and Chinese data, for example, are relatively strict. You will need to understand these rules and how they apply to the data you hold.

For some of these fields, this is reasonably obvious. Capturing a customer's name, address, or date of birth may have valid reasons for your reporting, but details of disabilities or medical history may not.

Where this becomes more difficult is in "free-text" fields, in which colleagues (or customers themselves) have entered in text to provide a description. This text could include highly sensitive customer data.

We must assess what data we have captured as an organisation, what we are using for reporting, what access we will give our colleagues to this data and how we control this access, and how we will manage this data in the future.

6.7.3   Data Bias

Bias in data is usually only obvious in hindsight. The individual steps that lead to the bias are not often purposely biased, instead seeming logical choices.

Commonly, even global companies will create functions centred around one office or region. An engineering function may work out of one office, and the analytics function out of another. Such office-based teams can help teams work together better, can help integrate new colleagues faster and ensure everyone is getting support in the team.

However, in doing so, many teams often become much less diverse, and this lack of diversity can lead to data issues. In one sector of society, whether this is specific to a gender, culture or any other sector, certain attitudes or biases may be inherent, and not understood to be a bias by the people themselves.

Processes within a company that were build many years ago also may hold bias, for example, if one gender was historically associated as the primary account holder on a mortgage, then this may skew reporting of mortgage holders if we don't understand the bias that was inherent when this data was collected.

Whilst ensuring we have a diverse workforce, we cannot rely on this to ensure our processes are not biased. Instead, we must remind colleagues working both in our engineering and analytics teams of the pitfalls of not addressing bias within our work.

Example: Bias in Action
In 2014, Amazon built a machine-learning system for recruitment. This tool would scan the CVs of candidates and select the ones that should be hired.

Within a year a problem had been identified. The tool was only selecting men.

The problem was caused by the data this model was based on. They had scanned resumes collected over the past 10 years, which had predominantly been male. The machine-learning model had taught itself that women, or more specifically, references to women, such as "women's chess team" or a "women's college" were negative impacts and was penalising them, so they would not be identified as suitable candidates for the roles.

The company spent years trying to mitigate for these biases, and presumably others around ethnicity, location, age, etc. that we might expect could impact the results. Unable to build a neutral model, in 2018 Amazon gave up on this project.

6.8 Data Is Data

It is a commonly held belief that programming languages are akin to different countries' languages. This is not really the case. There are a few different types of programming languages, and within each type, the programming languages are more like different dialects of the same language.

There are many ways we can categorise programming languages, and one could fill an entire book with different categorisations and explanations. Below is a very simplified view of categorisation into the three categories of declarative, object-orientated, and procedural.

For the purposes of this book, we should think of declarative as being database and reporting languages, whilst object-oriented and procedural are application development languages (Fig. 6.5).

As you can see, there is overlap between the groups. Python and R are both declarative and object-orientated. This is because the languages can be used in different ways.

An engineer that has worked extensively with any one of the languages within each of the three groups will find it very easy to transition to another within the same group. The fundamental concepts between the individual languages within the groups do not change. Therefore, when an engineer needs to pick up a new system, they need only learn the new syntax, which is not likely to vary vastly, and additional functions that still work on the data in an expected way.

For a data and analytics team, we are likely to want to focus mostly on the declarative languages, unless we need to build an application. Because of the split in skills for these languages, this will probably mean we need different engineers with experience in those skills.

Perhaps even more important than this is the concept that "data is data", no matter what system you are querying it with. Fundamentally if you have two sets of data and you want to join them together you need to fully understand the implications of what will happen. How do we join or compare them? If you get this wrong, this will cause issues.

So, the concepts of how data and sets of data work together are much more important than knowing the syntax and functions of the languages, though certainly, knowing those in detail will help.

To see evidence of this in academia, universities will teach languages such as Java or Python on Bachelors and Masters engineering courses, and will not cover many of the other languages that are more likely to be employed in business. This is because they expect their students to be able to use the concepts with other languages relatively easily.

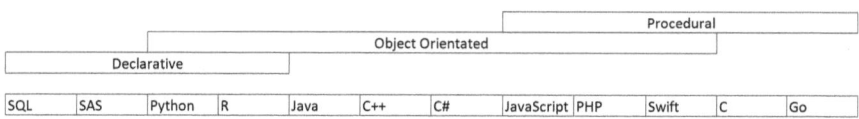

Fig. 6.5 Declarative, object-orientated, and procedural languages

This is also seen in qualifications such as the Microsoft Certified Engineer courses and exams (now named Azure after its infrastructure platform), in which students are no longer required to memorise the plethora of functions out there, instead only focussing on the concepts and being able to reference the formula syntax as they study and take the exams [2].

Hopefully this will change your opinion on what to look for in an engineer. Knowing every function in a language is not nearly as important as knowing the fundamental concepts of the language.

This same logic will also apply to many of the applications your team may use.

As an example of this, it is very common to use data visualisation tools such as Tableau, Power BI, or business objects. These applications are very easy to move between. They also require the same knowledge of concepts around how data works, so they can be thought of as in the same group as the declarative languages.

To quantify this transferability, I would expect an engineer/analyst with a firm grasp of data concepts and experience with one of these three visualisation tools, to be able to pick up the basics of another visualisation tool within a few hours and to be able to create more complex reporting within a day.

Data is data. No matter the language.

6.9   Chapter Summary

1. Data drives what your team can accomplish.
2. Calculations should be held as close to your base tables as possible.
3. Automation is essential.
4. Automation can be used to mitigate risk, communicate issues, and fix data problems.
5. Data is Data. What system or language you are using matters much less than your approach to how you manage data.

References

1. *Scikit Learn Python Libraries*. Fabian Pedregosa, Gael Varoquaux, Alexandre Gramfort and Vincent Michel, National Institute for Research in Digital Science and Technology (2011) https://scikit-learn.org/
2. *Exam AZ-204: Developing Solutions for Microsoft Azure*. Microsoft Certifications. (2021) https://docs.microsoft.com/en-us/learn/certifications/exams/az-204

Chapter 7
Stakeholders

7.1 Understanding and Pre-empting the Business

In order to know how to design a report, the report designer needs to understand what the report is going to be used for and how it is going to be used.

It is not enough to just get requirements from the business.

Section 7.2.1 discusses how we should approach finding out what a stakeholder needs, rather than just what they want. However, more important than this is our ability to pre-empt what a stakeholder will need in future.

In some organisations, it can take up to a year to source data from source system, especially for those from Sect. 6.2.1. A new report may take several months from requirements gathering, through build, testing, and release. Because of this, we need to think ahead.

What is the business likely to want from us?

The only way we can know this is to ensure we understand what is happening in the business, and keep up to date with how the business and its challenges are evolving.

In many larger organisations, central reporting functions will service a huge range of different business areas. In these cases, we should still work on ensuring the reporting designers do gain business knowledge; albeit at a lesser depth of knowledge and for more areas.

At this point, it can be tempting to create specialisation in your team, so you have each team member learning a different part of the business. Section 3.3 may persuade you otherwise.

When a change request is raised to add in a new field or element to a report or dataset, you should challenge yourself and your team as to why you didn't foresee this. A later chapter, Sect. 8.7 deals with the detail of how to do this.

J. Mackay, *From Data to Insights*, https://doi.org/10.1007/978-981-96-3545-0_7

This is where you and your teams experience in knowing what reporting is likely to be asked for becomes very useful. It will be obvious that an internal colleague report might need to have a company structure included in which to filter to different departments, but have you considered identifying which colleagues are in which country, which are working from home or have certain expertise?

Whether you choose to have this amount of detail in the report or not, facilitating this in your data will enable your team to quickly add it in to the reporting should you be asked later on. We can also save time and effort for our engineers if we ensure that all of this work is done when these tables are originally created, so rework at a later date is avoided.

7.2   Stakeholder Management

7.2.1   Stakeholder Requirements

What your stakeholders think they need, and what they actually need is rarely the same thing.

In the same way your strategy needed to be dealt with by starting at the end goal and working backwards, so your stakeholder requirements will need to work the same way.

Don't start by asking what reporting your stakeholders want.

Why?
When you ask a stakeholder exactly what they want, they will have pre-conceptions about what they can get.
This will limit the vision of what your stakeholders can imagine, and you will likely be asked to provide the types of reporting they already receive.
This will then be more difficult to sell your vision of your end strategy.

If I had asked people what they wanted, they would have said faster horses.
—Heny Ford, President Ford Motor Company

It's really hard to design products by focus groups. A lot of times, people don't know what they want until you show it to them.
—Steve Jobs, CEO Apple Inc.

Instead ask:

1. What questions do they want to answer?
2. What problems they have that need answering?
3. What challenges do they have?
4. What are they missing in what they get now?

There will of course be exceptions to this rule. Regulatory or financial reports being provided in a set format, or even very particular senior managers, will set strict guidelines for what reporting is created. However, this still leaves the structure of the data and analytics processes to be designed.

When requirements have been gathered and the first draft of the report created, there will inevitably be changes required.

What you are also likely to encounter are "additional-asks". These can range from and extra field in a report or an additional tab to something so fundamental that it means starting the piece of work again from scratch.

Whilst we will never be free of this difficulty, we can put into place steps that will minimise their frequency and impact.

7.2.2 Requirement's Framework

A framework for requirements gathering must balance the capturing of new requirements comprehensively against ease of stakeholder engagement.

Without detailed requirements, reporting will be developed that does not answer the right questions or perform the right calculations, and your team will also spend too much time interpreting and guessing what the stakeholder has asked for.

With too much bureaucracy, stakeholders will be put off engaging your team, and your reporting will no longer quickly fall out of date with business changes and become irrelevant. End users may also start to create their own reporting, combining what they can get from you and transforming it themselves.

7.2.3 Collaboration

For more complex requirements, such as the development of a new report, or reporting from a new system, a particularly useful tool is that of a workshop, or even collaborative report creation.

As businesses move towards more collaborative tools, such as Skype, Teams, Lync, and Web-ex, we can enable our analysts to work directly with our stakeholders and have a conversation on the requirements to ensure a full understanding of what is needed and possible.

One step on from this is collaborative report creation, in which your team develops parts of new reports or report changes in collaborative sessions. Through these sessions, a great deal of time can be saved in preventing the need for iterative report changes, misunderstandings in requirements, and being able explain complex ideas more easily.

Regular meetings between your analysts and key business stakeholders provide a platform to facilitate better collaboration. These should be in addition to workshops progressing individual pieces of work. Potentially a shared action log can be kept and regularly maintained which are used on these calls to talk through the ongoing actions and upcoming development. This can also provide a great way in understanding the prioritisation the business would like to place on your team's actions, which in turn helps to identify where your team can better add benefit… so long as all these actions support your team's overall strategy!

Management level meetings should also be held regularly, though potentially with a lower frequency, with key senior stakeholders. Through these, the high-level actions and broad strokes of what your team is progressing can be discussed, and more distant changes being anticipated by your stakeholders discussed.

7.2.4   Show, Don't Tell

When presenting questions or ideas to your stakeholders, it is usually best to visualise this for them with an example.

Rather than asking the stakeholder what categorisation they want to assign to a dropdown list in a source system, instead provide them with the complete dropdown list, with suggestions that you have come up with (Fig. 7.1).

This will give the stakeholder an immediate indication of what you are wanting from them, reducing the amount of work they have to do to get the full list of options, and also showing them how easy it is, which may encourage them to provide the answers more quickly.

When a new idea, report, tool, or functionality is demonstrated to your stakeholders, as well as doing this collaboratively, we must also consider what questions are being asked of the stakeholders, what input we are expecting and what outcome we are seeking.

7.2.5   Accountability

When the goal of your stakeholder management has changed from waiting for report or change requests to be provided, to Sect. 7.1 and ensuring your team's goals support the business, and your data infrastructure is comprehensive, adaptable and supports future development, then engagement with your stakeholders becomes much easier.

Complaint System Dropdown	Suggested Group
customer didn't receive everything they expected to get	Process
customer unhappy with advice received	Service
business processed the customer's request incorrectly	Process
customer unhappy with fees or charges	Product
took too long to get answered	Service
unhappy with product offered	Process

Fig. 7.1 Example of suggested grouping

These principles will drive a great relationship with your key business areas. However, we can't expect everything to be plain sailing.

There is great value in being candid, acting accountable and taking responsibility.
—Bob Iger, Disney CEO

It is very important that data issues created by your own team, as well as others, failed changes, reporting errors, and mistakes are not ignored. In admitting to these, it forces you and your team to think carefully about what has gone wrong, and consider how these can be prevented in future.

For major issues, stakeholders should be notified immediately. In the Sect. 6.5, we discussed ways we can achieve this with no additional overheads to our team.

We can, however, build on this. A great way to do this is to send out regular communication out to our stakeholders or business with the list of issues encountered that month, number of reports impacted, how long it took to resolve, who/what caused the fault and mitigations put in place to prevent this happening again. Through this you may wish to include a metric to show what percentage of reports were issued in SLA, and how many were issued.

The inclusion of such metrics into a regular report allows you to turn this into positive promotion for the team, which for data and analytics teams that do not gain much exposure, can be very hard to achieve. It also facilitates a platform to describe future developments, or even to explain how something works in the data infrastructure or reporting.

7.3 Waterfall and Agile Project Management

7.3.1 Waterfall

Waterfall project management [1] is the traditional approach to project management.

With this approach, distinct phases of a project are mapped out and worked through sequentially. Following this, a project progresses through the full lifecycle of the project, from planning through to completion before any product is presented to the stakeholders and end users.

Waterfall methodology offers a team a chance to make a big-gang at the end of development of a new product, where the release is of something completely new and unseen, and the product will be finalised and polished.

The problems with this approach arise because the end users or the product won't know what they are going to get until the end of the project. If what has been specified in requirements gathering at the start isn't as then envisioned. Additionally, when requirements change mid-point through a project, it can be very hard to cater for this in the project plan.

7.3.2   Agile

Agile project management [2] is a form of project management in which a project is split into segments to enable faster distribution of reporting to the stakeholders. These segments are called "sprints".

Within reporting, this is done by separating out various parts of a new report, and as soon as one part is ready, providing this to the stakeholder, then starting work on the next part of the report and adding this on to the initial report, then working on the next, etc.

At the end of each sprint, the stakeholder has the opportunity to see if the requirements have been met, and the progress can be more readily amended. If the requirements have not been met, then less time has been expended going down the wrong path.

So, the project becomes more agile.

This style of project management does have drawbacks. It will require more time testing the reporting, as this needs to be done at the end of each sprint. The stakeholders will also see a much less polished version of the report initially, which will not work for all audiences. Finally, documentation is often written at the start and not rewritten for each sprint or left until the end, and so is either not available for reference in early or later iterations of the project.

However, it will deliver a product more quickly and can save a great deal of time in the development of new reports.

7.4   Engagement

There are two types of engagement we walk to talk about. The one you are probably thinking about is how your team can be engaged. That is the next chapter. This chapter is how you can stay engaged with what's going on. It's much more important.

Fully automated reporting, or at least as automated as possible, is the goal of most teams as discussed in the Sect. 6.5. However, this creates a problem with knowing what is going on in your business area.

Having visibility of what is going on in the business, and being engaged with upcoming initiatives and changes is a key component of what will make your team work.

Quite often the changes that will impact you the most are not the ones other business areas would expect. A change in process can easily stop a report from working as intended. To understand this, it going to be best to see some examples of issues I have seen arise from business changes.

1. Weekend working in a telephony call centre.
2. Operational time savings in a work logging tool.

To do this you are going to need to have representation on the right calls. Not only this, but you will need the right people on these calls.

Most operational areas will have regular catchups with the senior management, change calls to discuss upcoming amendments to process and challenges and project calls to tackle the larger implementations for the business. If they don't, they should.

The representative who is attending these calls from your team should send on a summary of any actions your team needs to undertake and important changes to the business and send it on. Potentially this could go to all, or the senior portion of your team.

This note taking has a few benefits. Firstly, it ensures your representative is paying attention and really listening to what is going on. Secondly, it means you need fewer people on that call. Thirdly, it allows more of your team to be engaged in what is going on in the business.

The spanner in the works for your engagement can often be the business or operation itself.

If you are an external team to the area you support, you may be seen as an outsider, or service provider and so there will be an expectation that and changes that could occur will be raised with your team formally through a change request.

I will go out on a limb and say this is not possible. There must be regular conversations about ongoing activities and changes between your team and the area you support.

Without this, you will not have any indication that your reporting could have been impacted, and so issues may not go noticed for days, weeks, or even months.

7.5   Change Requests

The ubiquitous "change request" often forms the mainstay of a reporting team's incoming work. How we handle them will completely change how the team operates, the amount and type of work coming in, the relationships both within the team and those we have with stakeholders, how much value we add to the business and how good our reporting is.

There are various ways in which we can enable the wider business to engage our reporting team with change requests.

At one end of this spectrum, the business will simply contact whoever they want in the team to carry out the work and this team member just gets on with it. We will call this an "Open" change request system.

At the other end of the spectrum, the business must engage the reporting team through a change request form, which is then managed as a project. Requirements gathered, potentially funds required or quotes requested, stakeholders engaged, meetings setup and colleagues assigned, regular updates to all stakeholders undertaken and documentation created, maintained and presented. We will call this a "Closed" change request system.

However, we should not think of this as a binary decision, instead as a spectrum. Somewhere in the middle is usually where we want the change request process to be.

To understand both ends of the spectrum more, we will look at the advantages and disadvantages of both.

7.5.1   Open Advantages

Easy to engage. Stakeholders don't have to worry about how to engage you.

No hurdles. Stakeholders know that all have to do is send a message.

Stakeholders have no barriers to engaging your team.

Stakeholders build a close rapport with your team.

Usually faster changes. A small change can be carried out in minutes.

No management overheads. Your team managers won't have to spend time on this process.

Colleagues become very specialised in fewer reports.

7.5.2   Open Disadvantages

Stakeholders have the opportunity to leave change requests to the last minute.

Very difficult to track the volume of changes coming into your team.

Very difficult to manage the workloads of the team.

Stakeholders may not approach the best suited colleague.

No formal requirements gathering, so changes tend to be very iterative.

Without change control, report changes are more prone to have errors.

Best practice not enforced, so poorer reliability and consistency.

Inconsistent experience for stakeholders from different members of your team.

Fewer colleagues have expertise in each report.

7.5.3   Closed Advantages

Requirements gathering is very comprehensive, and few iterations are required.

Easier to manage team workload.

Fewer change requests come into team as stakeholders put off by process.

All changes are well controlled and tested. Fewer implementation issues.

Reporting code at a better standard, so lower ongoing maintenance.

Reporting looks better as more time taken to polish each report.

More aligned reporting.

Impact of changes better scoped, leading to fewer issues.

Makes it easier for stakeholders to track where a request is up to.

7.5.4 Closed Disadvantages

Team becomes irrelevant as stakeholders look for alternatives rather than getting team to update or create new reports.

Logic and processes may become out of date as other teams reluctant to go through rigorous change process.

Changes take too long, business left with requirements unsatisfied for long periods.

Management of the change process requires significant time/effort.

Team takes shortcuts with process as it is too onerous.

Senior stakeholders may expect this to be done for them, and so benefits are not realised.

Change process may require additional access for forms and can create more barriers.

Minor changes are not requested, so small faults start to arise in reporting.

Cottage industries are created in stakeholder teams to avoid using your team.

The disadvantages of both the open and closed extreme of the change request spectrum both outweigh the advantages.

Because of this, either one should be avoided unless absolutely essential.

Instead, a happy medium should be sought, which will depend entirely on the type of changes your team receives, how many, the complexity, who your stakeholders, the size of your team, and the importance of speed over accuracy.

Over the next few sections of the book, we will discuss more subjects that must be taken into consideration for your change request process.

7.6 Change Management

Change is the most common way for reporting to go wrong.

Either through unintended consequences, poorly scoped requirements, lack of or not thorough enough testing, poor communication or even poor timing.

Because of this, in addition to the way changes are scoped for stakeholder requirements and engaged through change requests, also the way changes are scoped, implemented, and communicated needs to be very thoroughly considered.

In July 2024, third party software from the company CrowdStrike, which was a cybersecurity service and formed part of the Microsoft Azure suite of applications, had an update.

The small update that was sent out went wrong, creating a global IT outage which impacted airlines, hospitals, banks, and even emergency services (Fig. 7.2).

The fault was not just from CrowdStrike who created the update, but also on Microsoft for not testing the updates they allowed to be implemented.

Changes need to be peer reviewed. Every time.

Fig. 7.2 Microsoft-CrowdStrike Global IT outage (https://commons.wikimedia.org/wiki/
File:CrowdStrike_BSOD_at_LGA.jpg)

Peer reviewing performs three functions:

1. Improved testing of changes. Having a second colleague look over a report increases the chances of errors being caught before a report is sent out to stakeholders.
2. Peer-pressure. More rigorous testing by the colleague creating the change, as they are aware their team members will be checking their work.
3. Increased cross-skilling within the team as a second team member then learns what is in the report.

Within the team, peer reviews can be further bolstered by having two reviewers for more complex changes. One to review one element of the report, possibly the data and logic, and one to review the report functionality, visuals and to compare against another report or source system.

Within the peer review, it is a good idea to set up a framework for what needs checking. When a peer review is completed, this list provides the basis for what this colleague is agreeing they have completed.

For some reporting teams, the stakeholder is the expert in the data, and your colleagues may not have the expertise to fully test a report. In this case, it's a good idea to involve your stakeholders in this testing. This can bring better collaboration with your stakeholders and works particularly well with operational reporting teams or centralised reporting teams that report on several different types of functions.

For changes to existing processes or reports, it can be very difficult to review a change and work out what is different. To overcome this, the old version of the report should be refreshed at the same time as the new report is created and prepared for testing. This allows for side-by-side testing of the change. It is much easier to spot an issue when outputs are compared against another report. However, when this is done, the team should ensure that the data is also compared against the source system or data, as potentially both reports could be wrong.

For key reports, side-by-side testing of the original report against the new report for a period of time allows potential issues to be spotted that are either infrequent, or only arise at certain times, such as rolling over a week or month end. Enable side-by-side changes is not always easy when they use the same source dataset, and the change involves an amendment to the base data. In this case, a development environment can be created, or just a complete copy of the base dataset.

Backout plans are essential for any changes. Usually these are quite simply the process of saving the original code/logic, or backing up the dataset before the change is made. This can be made much easier with a by-design process in which reports and processes are regularly backed up.

Sometimes immediate changes need to be made to the processes or reports that are not ideal. These temporary fixes are usually imposed by senior stakeholders or essential and unforeseen obligations. When these are undertaken, it is important that they are followed up by a well-controlled version of the change in which more time can be taken. When this is the case, stakeholders should be informed of the reduced controls being implemented on this change and also that your team provides estimates for the time it will take to complete the comprehensive fix later on activity.

A final consideration should be the time and day on which change implementations are made.

If the team's reporting works on a weekly cycle, or there are days in which more important reports are sent out, then changes should be made to reports to take this into consideration. For many teams, a Monday will be the most important day. In this case, changes should never be made on a Friday, as the team would not have time to backout a change. This can be compounded further if lengthy testing is required, so potentially changes should only be made on a Tuesday, with Wednesday to Friday available for testing and backing out the change if required.

7.7 Documentation

Documentation is great, but it also often gets avoided by teams and treated as red-tape that isn't really necessary.

However, documentation can reduce queries coming to your team, improve reports, make changes easier and less likely to go wrong, help with absence, as well as many more expected and unexpected benefits.

When we talk about documentation, there are several types we should consider, and all are essential.

1. Job-cards are the most commonly thought of pieces of documentation. For manual reporting, how the report is run. This is a great tool to allow other colleagues to pick up a manual process.
2. Cover sheets on a report can have many components each of which can be a great addition:

    (a) Provide a consistent "brand" for your team's reports.
    (b) Makes it extremely easy for report users to find information on the report.
    (c) Capture who to contact when there is an issue.
    (d) Capture what changes have gone into the report and when.
    (e) Show a version number, aiding in conversations with your stakeholders.
    (f) Explain what a report's purpose is, so metrics are not misconstrued.
    (g) Show what systems a report runs from.
    (h) Show report frequency and timings.
    (i) Include a last report refresh date. This can be done automatically.
    (j) Provide other information such as future updates and changes.
    (k) Facilitate feedback and change requests within the report itself.
    (l) Exception reporting can be included to identify potential problems in the report.

3. Documenting the peer review and stakeholder review creates an ownership and puts extra responsibility on the peer reviewer to ensure it is thoroughly tested. This can also be included on the cover sheet of the report.
4. Definition page or tab of a report allows the report user an easy-to-find definition of every metric or field and can include the lookup tables for hierarchies used in the logic or additional information about certain elements.
5. Change logs allow the team to not only track what, when, who, and why changes are implemented, but also allow the managers of the team to use these lists in communications out to the stakeholders to show what work is being done. This usually helps in team performance reviews.
6. Code comments written into the base logic of a report are usually only seen by the team's engineers and analysts and provide a great way to explain what each section of code/logic does, which makes both testing and future changes much easier, quicker, and less prone to error.
7. Stakeholder requirements for new requests and change requests should be documented and saved. This is particularly important for regulatory, financial and high priority reporting.

Ideally all of these above types of documentation should be undertaken in a reporting team.

All offer great benefit to the team, and though may seem like a large overhead when they are first implemented, once embedded into a team provide benefits that far outweigh the costs.

7.8 Team Representation

Reporting and especially data are often an afterthought.

Within senior management, there is often a lack of understanding, knowledge, and expertise in reporting and more so data. Even within the senior management of reporting teams, there is a lack of understanding of data.

This makes for a huge issue for us.

Data and reporting should be some of the first two considerations when making business decisions and changes, and so you will need to ensure that you have representation on forums and meetings in which any business changes or decisions might arise.

Additionally, by having data and analytics representation on their calls, the business will have an expert available to answer questions on where to find reporting, or how to use a particular report. The representative can also understand the context for requests that are being made for the data and analytics teams, instead of relying won what has been provided on a change-form or e-mail.

7.9 Chapter Summary

1. Avoid quick wins at all costs. Make sure any development supports your long-term strategy.
2. Be on change calls, senior management catchups, and new project calls.
3. The framework for requirements and engagement to your team defines how effective reports will be.
4. Ensure requirements encapsulate future requests as well as what the stakeholder need right now.
5. Collaborative teams work through understanding and regular contact.

References

1. *Prince 2 Project Management.* Projects In Controlled Environments (2021) https://www.prince2.com
2. *Agile project management.* Association For Project Management (2021) https://www.apm.org.uk

Chapter 8
Reporting and Insight

8.1 Choosing Reporting Tools

There are numerous tools that can be used for data and analytics. Choosing the right one, or ensuring your team is currently using the best one for the job can be deceiving.

The majority of small reporting teams in businesses solely use Microsoft Excel for their data storage and reporting. It's a great broad-spectrum tool, but it does have issues without proper controls.

During the Coronavirus pandemic, the UK government carried out its data collection, processing and reporting using Excel. Excel is a fantastic tool, but has limitations. One of its limits is in how many records can be stored on one tab.

For the UK government, this limitation became a massive issue. As the numbers of records added to the data tab in their Excel workbook, exceeded the maximum row number of 1,048,476, then additional records just weren't included.

When the reporting team realised the issue, they were able to resolve it, by using a second data tab. But by then, then erroneous data had been issued by the government and circulated around the world. It was an embarrassing lesson in using the wrong tool for the job [1, 2].

A comprehensive explanation of the attributes of a single reporting tool would be a book unto itself. There are also far too many tools out there to detail here, so we will focus on just a few of the most commonly used tools.

J. Mackay, *From Data to Insights*, https://doi.org/10.1007/978-981-96-3545-0_8

8.1.1   Microsoft Excel/Google Documents/Apache OpenOffice

It is unlikely you have not encountered one or more of these products. They all provide a quick and easy way to bring data into a tool, from which you can readily perform calculations on and create great visualisations.

Flexibility, ease of use, as well as being understood by almost everybody even at just a basic level, means that these tools are ideal for creating reporting.

When delivering a finished reporting product, it is not ideal to store the data in these tools; however, as many issues will be encountered in keeping data consistent, ensuring formulas are applied to the entire dataset (especially new data), and automation of such a product is difficult.

Most similar tools have the ability to use a language such as VBA to create some automation within the tool. Whilst this can be a benefit, this functionality is often used instead of more complex formulas or tools, and generally it is better to avoid using this functionality where possible.

Functionally and visually, Excel and similar tools can create amazing reporting (Fig. 8.1).

These dashboards can connect to a variety of data sources, such as SQL, SAS, Hadoop, Web Services, and many more. By storing our data in a more controlled tool such as these, and utilising excel for solely the reporting, we can leverage the benefits of both systems.

Fig. 8.1 An interactive colleague schedule dashboard in excel

8.1.2   *Tableau*

Tableau [3] is a very powerful reporting tool that has the ability to pull data in from a variety of data sources and present this in very customisable dashboards (Fig. 8.2).

The dashboards created in Tableau can be interactive, with the end user able to change parameters of what is being viewed.

When bringing data in to Tableau, this data can then be transformed with calculations and manipulation of the data. The benefits of this are that data from different systems can be combined, however for a data and analytics team, I would suggest moving the manipulation of data, to the data layer in a server or dedicated data tool where possible, as data control and governance can be challenging.

Tableau stores the data it reports on within the tool, which improves the performance of the visualisations, but means that generally the desktop tool will be rolled out to end users, and can require more storage and processing power.

Access to the data and analytics can be controlled through the tool.

When compared to similar products, Tableau falls at the midrange for ease of use. There is certainly a learning curve to using this tool, and it is recommended to get specialist training for your team in using this software.

The final consideration of Tableau is cost. The pricing options for Tableau can often make it cheap for a small team with few report users, but when scaled up, it can be expensive due to a per-user plan, though investigation of the options available to your team are required as this may well have changed.

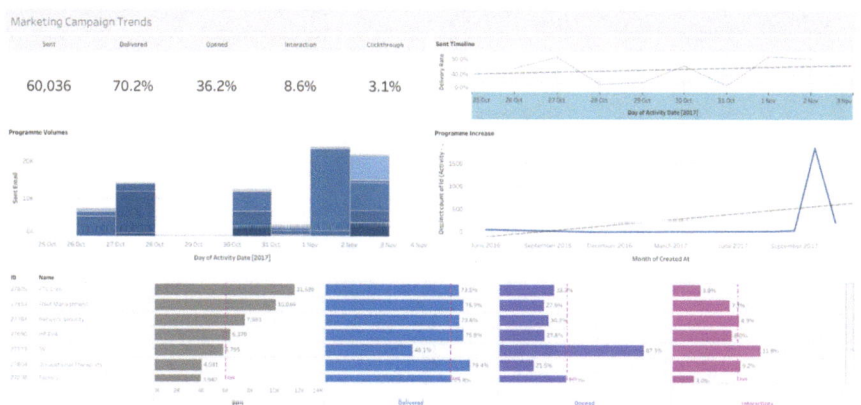

Fig. 8.2 Tableau example report

8.1.3   Business Objects

Business Objects [4] is another very powerful reporting tool, though differs in its approach to most other reporting tools by splitting out the data transformation layer and visual presentation layer into separate tools.

Within the Designer tool, a data "universe" is created in which data can be manipulated, and relationships created through which to report on. The visualisation Webi tool then provides the ability to create graphics, which can look pretty good, though not on the same level as Tableau.

Business Objects doesn't store any data in its data layer, which differs to tableau; however, the way of transforming data is largely the same. By splitting out the data layer into a separate tool, Business Objects does provide better data control, though again it is still recommended to perform as much of the data transformation in a dedicated tool such as a SQL or SAS server (Fig. 8.3).

In some situations, Business Objects can be "fiddlier" to get working; however, this is fairly similar to the learning curve of Tableau. Most users will prefer the one they are more familiar with.

Some of the concepts in facilitating data drill-throughs are not the easiest to get a hang of, and as with Tableau, training is well worth while investing in, especially for engineers and analysts that will be building the data "universe" as well as the reporting visuals.

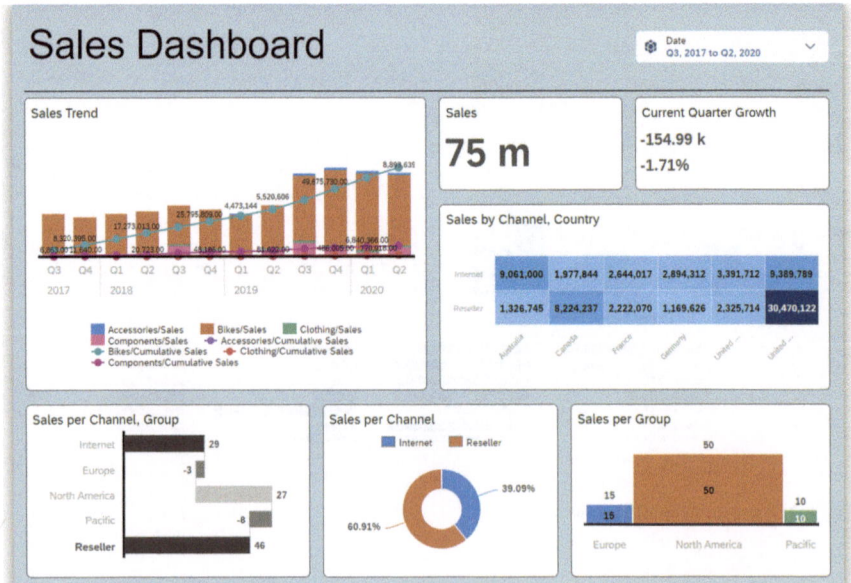

Fig. 8.3 Business Objects example report

Business Objects is most commonly used through a browser, (though older versions did use a desktop tool) which can make the distribution of end user reporting easier.

Access to the data and analytics can be controlled through the tool.

Pricing options can be easier to manage for larger deployments, as per instance licences are available. Though again this may have changed.

8.1.4 Power BI

Power BI [5] is a more recent tool than the long-established Business Objects and Tableau.

More akin to Tableau, Power BI has its data transformation and visualisations in one tool; however, the options available are much more basic.

Power BI has the option to bring data into it, or to read data directly from the data source. However direct data queries are much more difficult to setup, unless your team already utilises an Azure database (Fig. 8.4).

Creation of reporting in Power BI is extremely easy, and great looking visuals can be set up almost immediately. The ease of use of Power BI can mean that an analyst who is relatively experienced in other reporting tools could start building reports without any dedicated training. For those who do need training, it's a much easier tool to learn than Tableau or Business Objects.

However, with this very intuitive functionality, comes a very limited ability to customise visuals, and so building reports can change from "what do we need" to "what can we build".

Fig. 8.4 Power BI example report

Distribution of reporting is where Power BI can really shine, when your business uses other Microsoft products. Inbuilt integration into Microsoft SharePoint and Microsoft Teams makes it very easy to showcase interactive reporting in tools that are often used by businesses, removing the barrier of having to install additional tools to view reports, or sending out non-interactive reports.

8.2   The End of Ad-Hoc Reports

Ad-hoc reporting is not inevitable.

In the Sect. 7.2, we discussed the metric for assessing your own team of a "Reports within SLA %", and sharing this with your stakeholders.

The "number of ad-hoc reports" your team produces should also be a metric. The more you produce, the worse your reporting capability is.

This will not be the case for all teams, sometimes, a reporting team is constrained by the framework they work within, and their roles responsibilities. In these cases, the metric should instead be the "number of requests than required complex analysis".

As ad-hoc request is a request for additional work to be carried out by your team to either supplement an existing report, or provide data or metrics on something new.

The question you should be asking when an ad-hoc request comes in is why don't your reports already give this detail? Why has no-one thought to create a report that already answers that question?

8.2.1   Detail, Detail, Detail

Reports should contain detail. We can design reports to give a huge amount of detail, accessed when a user hovers over, drills down or double clicks on a number. In doing so, we can give the end user the ability to validate what numbers they are seeing, or to check which cases make up a population.

This empowers the end user to be able to answer their own questions immediately, without having to engage your team for more detail, or to waste their own time.

One of the main reasons for an ad-hoc request is to find out what is happening in another report. The request for this additional detail might not even mention the first report they were looking at. This poses an unforeseen issue for your team, the ad-hoc request you produce then needs to match what they end user has already seen. Of course, with a great data infrastructure, this will be much easier, but can you be certain you have provided a data set with the same filters enabled, products selected, etc?

By providing the additional detail in the report, these queries are never raised.

8.2.2   Comprehensive Reporting

Our reporting should cover as wide an area of the business as possible. When we are requested to provide a financial overview or one product area, why not provide this for all product areas, with a button or slicer on to select the filter the end user wants.

The answer might be that we don't want every user seeing every area. In this case, you can do more in your data layer to support this. Through most reporting tools, reporting can show the user only specific areas associated with their area.

8.2.3   Date Periods

A very common problem in reporting is to have multiple reports, each one showing a different time period for the same data. Whilst this is an issue that cannot be resolved in PDFs, images, or e-mails, this is an issue in that can be resolved in most reporting tools including Excel.

As Excel is the worst culprit for this, we will take a look at how this can be resolved in the data, which will then give additional functionality in the report.

The first step is to create several versions of the data and join them together for each date period we want to look at. This way, data that is in two or more date periods, such as the current week and current month will be duplicated, but older data that may only be in one date period will only be shown once.

This data is then presented in Excel through pivot tables, which gives Excel some great interactive capabilities.

Within Excel, we can then use slicers to control the pivots (Fig. 8.5).

Fig. 8.5 An Excel report using slicers to control date periods

As in the example above, we can use the same pivots and charts to show different date periods, and go even further to report at a different level for each period. You may want to see the previous week at a daily level, but previous 4 weeks at a weekly level, and the previous 12 months at a monthly level. This technique gives you this option.

You may also notice in this example that the metric type of "Actual Duration (Hours/Mins)" and "Original Duration" can be changed with a slicer. This allows a different view of the data to be included in the same report.

In the example shown, the user can also double click on any number in the pivot to show the underlying data at a very low level.

8.2.4   From Ad-Hoc to Change Request

When ad-hoc requests are raised that are requesting additional detail to an existing report, rather than creating a new version of this report with the additional detail in, every effort should be made to convert this ad-hoc request into a change request for the existing report.

In doing so, we can include this new piece of detail/slicer or element in an existing report.

This will have the benefits of providing the customer with the ability to have access to this additional detail at any point in the future, allowing other users of the report to view this additional detail and reduced requirement gathering for the change, as the existing report already contains all the other filters required.

8.2.5   Summarisation

Having multiple summarisations of the same data source in most reporting tools leads to only a very small increase in file size and allows very different views to be shown.

For some stakeholders, it is much easier to provide different visualisations, than to add too many different slicers and options into a report. This tends to be true for stakeholders that have less understanding of the processes being represented by the reporting, and those who would not normally interact with your reporting.

Summaries like this can work well, but be careful when pre-filtering data for the end user, that this is immediately obvious in that part of the report.

Summary reports should be comprehensive and have the ability to be viewed in isolation without needing the context of the rest of the report to understand them. This will allow end users to reference these sections without needing to refer back to any other reporting, or for these summarisations to be included in e-mails or other communications more easily.

8.2.6 Ongoing Support

By implementing the initiatives in the Chap. 7, your relationship with your stakeholders will already facilitate a much better understanding of upcoming additional requests and changes that can support the business; however, there is more we can do to ensure our reports are working well.

Keep on asking how it the reporting is being used. Regular check-ups with your stakeholders to see how they are using a specific report, if anything is missing from the report, if they are having any issues, or if they are doing anything else with the report, such as amending it, or extracting data for something else.

This will not only keep your reports up to date, but can also identify "cottage-industries" popping up as discussed in the Sect. 2.1.

To maintain this, a report checking schedule may be a useful way for your team to keep track of which reports have been checked, when, who with, and how regularly.

8.3 Predicting Issues

Many of the points discussed in this section are progressions from the data controls discussed in the Sect. 6.6, so ensure you are familiar with those approaches first.

8.3.1 Exception Reporting

Identifying issues in the base data when it arrives can allow alerts to be sent to teams responsible for those problems; however, we still need to make the report users aware of these issues within the reports themselves.

Alerts can be built into reports to highlight to the end users, issues that are impacting the report. This will add extra motivation to the responsible teams/colleagues to fix these issues, as well as providing the end user detail on what might not be correct in the report when they are using the report.

For more major errors, such as source systems not having refreshed data, error messages can be included at the top of reports. In most cases when a source system's data is not up to date, you would not want to publish the report; however, if the source system is secondary to the functioning of the report, then this may be a valid option.

8.3.2 Conditional Formatting

Within data tables, conditional formatting can be used to highlight erroneous values.

Fields not being populated, incorrect values or dates being entered into source systems can easily be flagged, will allow the end user to handle those entries appropriately.

As with the Sect. 8.3.1, it also provides additional motivation for the responsible team/colleague to rectify this issue.

Highlighting new values in a report can also be a very useful technique. The best way to approach this is to identify new values in the data layer, and add an additional flag onto the report, by which to trigger conditional formatting from.

8.3.3 Size Increases

Over time, you should anticipate that many categories of reporting will increase.

There may be an increase in the number of products reported on, colleagues reflected in a report, or dates visualised.

For any element that can increase in size, there will be a potential for visuals, pivots, or tables to overlap, which in some cases will cause errors and prevent the reports from refreshing.

8.3.4 Benchmarks and Targets

Benchmarks and targets can and will change. When this happens, conditional formatting and other elements of the reporting will need to be updated.

Embedding these targets into conditional formatting calculation fields can make updates to the report very time consuming.

To make this easier, these targets can be included as a new field in the report, which means that fewer changes are need to update them, and so fewer mistakes have the potential of being made.

For a much more comprehensive solution, these targets can be loaded into a table on your server, and then referenced in your report code to be used in your report. This will allow centralised changes to be very easily made to reporting, which will cascade down to all impacted reports, and mean that reporting changes will not be required.

8.4 Quick-Wins

Quick-wins, tactical solutions, short-term strategy, and interim measures are all terms for the same immediate response to a problem.

Quick wins are rarely quick wins. Instead, they:

1. Waste time.
2. Engender "work-around" culture.
3. Create "cottage industries".
4. Prevent you implementing a productive strategy.
5. Focus on symptoms not causes.
6. Make future changes more difficult.

Quick wins are the worst thing you can do to your team.

Every decision and step that your team makes must be towards and form part of your end strategy.

A quick win that you think will save time, but does not form part of your strategy will inevitably just make things worse.

Example: How a Quick Win Plays Out

Reporting Analyst Dave spends every Monday morning refreshing a report in Excel, then copying each tab to Power Point to be sent in a weekly pack. This is a task replicated in tens of thousands of reporting teams around the world.

You see the opportunity for the team engineer Jane to automate the step that creates the power point.

This is a quick win that will save Dave 30 min every day.

Let's see what happens…

You ask Jane to engage with Dave to automate the production of the power point slides.

Jane and Dave have a workshop in which they walk through the files required and any nuances in the way data is copied.

Jane starts work by using a very standard approach for this, creating VBA code to copy the content of the Excel workbook to PowerPoint.

At the end of Day 3, Jane has completed the task and sends it back to Dave for testing.

Dave tests the file, and realises some amendments need to be made. Because these are quite complex changes, he sends it back to Jane to complete.

Jane reworks the file and sends it back for further testing.

Dave tests the report and signs it off.

After 7 days FTE work you have saved Dave 30 min time a week. This is actually a good achievement, but there will be further consequences.

A few months later the next stage of your strategy is to have Jane change the queries in the Excel file to pull in more data so the Power Point can serve as a Monthly as well as Weekly report.

Days 8–9: Now when you ask Jane to make this amend, her estimated time to complete is increased from 1 day FTE to 2 days FTE, due to the increased complexity of the reporting which now includes VBA.

Day 10: Dave and Jane will then need to spend 1 day FTE together creating the new automated Monthly PowerPoint slides, which needs a collaborative approach due to different metrics being required on the PowerPoint (Dave's input) as well as VBA amendments (Jane's input)

A few months later and onto the next piece of your strategy, creating an interactive Excel dashboard to replace the PowerPoint slides, so the stakeholders can gain more insight from the reporting.

Days 11–16: Once again the task is been complicated by the automated VBA process, and so this task must once again be given to both Jane and Dave, due to the coding element and design element. This time, with the build of a completely new report, it will take 2 days FTE for Jane and 5 days FTE for Dave.

Each step of this process seems logical, but is complicated by the step before.

The overall time allocated was 9 days FTE for your engineer Jane and 9 days FTE for your analyst Dave.

By taking a step back and working out what the end goal would be, an interactive Excel dashboard, you could have saved 13 days FTE, and delivered the final product as quickly as your first release of an automated weekly PowerPoint was complete.

We have not taken into account any amendments to the report during this process would have taken far longer and ad-hoc granular extracts far longer.

This is a simplified example of the consequences of implementing "Quick-Wins".

An end-to-end strategy may involve 100–200 steps. For most teams, regular reporting will have to be maintained throughout this time. Any changes that are not part of this process will have a downstream impact the rest of the strategy.

To facilitate a successful long-term team creation or transition, the attitudes and goals of the team need to be aligned to your strategic goals. In terms of team ethos, by implementing "Quick Wins", we will deliver a message to our colleagues that they do not need to consider future changes, fault fixing or downstream impacts, and instead should just focus on the here and now.

It is incredibly important, that when one of your team is asked to undertake a piece of work, no matter how small, that they view it against the picture of the team's strategy.

This will serve two benefits, it will ensure that continuous work is being done to support this journey, but it will also ensure that when you get there, the team does not lapse back into old behaviours and practices.

A team that challenges practices and strives for improvements is one that will embody the ethos of "continuous improvement", which will help you not just reach your long-term goals, but lead a team that remains highly successful.

8.5 Executive Reporting

8.5.1 Supporting Reporting

Often, very bespoke views of data will be requested by executive audiences, to answer specific questions being raised, or key metrics for your business.

A common mistake is to build these graphics and executive reports without any supporting detail.

Whilst the report being distributed to the execs may only show a very high-level view of the reporting, we should always expect to be asked to validate these numbers, or add in further detail at short notice.

To facilitate this, any high-level metric should have a base report which can give a lower-level view of this data. Even if no-one will be actively using this lower-level report on a day-to-day basis, this will enable your team to react quickly, and will give you, your team and your stakeholders more confidence in the metrics being published.

8.5.2 Telling a Story

Report commentary is one of the most frequently misunderstood aspects of a reporting team.

Commentary should be the way of describing a pattern in the data that is not obvious or is unexpected. This insight should demonstrate how and why this is so, which will usually lead us to a solution of what needs to be remedied to either prevent this happening, or encouraging it to happen more.

Commentary is not insight (Fig. 8.6).

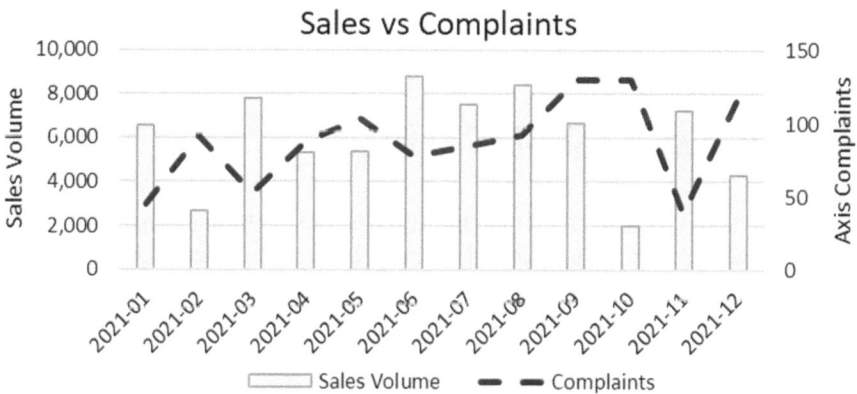

Fig. 8.6 Example of sales vs complaints chart

In the chart above, we will often find commentary ascribed to this that tells us what we can already see.

In December, the volume of complaints has increased by 300%, whilst the volume of sales has reduced by 59%.

This is not insightful. Even giving more detail to what we can see by explaining a lag between sales and complaints, and that the temporary dip in complaints in November was caused by a low sales volume in October, is not insightful.

What would be insightful, is to carry out analysis on what we can't see in this chart. For example:

- Did the dip in October sales cause the dip in November complaints?
- Explore the products sold over this period, how the complaint rates for each one?
- What was happening in the rest of the industry?
- Were there any external factors?

From these questions we can start to craft insight to inform our stakeholders on what they can't already see.

There is a next step to this. That is then trying to visualise this insight into the existing reporting, so this story doesn't need telling again, it can instead be presented in the regular reporting.

Is there something we can add into our existing charts, do we need to create a new one to track the impact of what we have identified in our insight?

When presenting this information, the charts and detail should be provided in a logical order. Usually this will be aligned to how the business progresses work.

For some examples, we might use these progressions:

- inputs → stock → outputs
- calls → capacity → quality → forecasts
- revenue → business costs → operating profit → net profit

This will be valid for trended charts, KPI scorecards, tables, or any other graphics.

Just remember, that if it doesn't add value, then it doesn't need to be there. Additionally, if there is too much information, then it will all be ignored.

8.6   I Want My Legacy to Be Insight

Insight is commonly at the top of the list of goals for a reporting team.

Insight will get the most focus and attention from senior stakeholders and is the most tangible and sellable achievement a reporting team can aspire to.

However, insight should never come first. There is a very good reason, it has been left until so late in this book and applies to insight-only teams as much as it does with reporting and insight teams.

The vast majority of work involved in creating insight is in the preparation of data. For this, there are differing approaches, which line up closely to the project management approaches of Sects. 7.3.1 and 7.3.2.

An agile approach as discussed in the Sect. 7.3 can yield insight outputs much quicker; however, this should be undertaken with caution. Because the bulk of work involved in insight is within the data, having to recut the data each time to support the insight outputs, means that the work involved is increased dramatically.

Where possible insight should be included in regular reporting.

Creating one-time insight packs is often the first point in creating insight and can often help in the creative process of the analyst. However, depending on the type of insight, it will often be the case that this insight will need to be refreshed, or would be more valuable if it was included in a regularly refreshed report, so changes in the conclusions of this insight can be seen.

8.6.1 So, What? Insight

It is not enough just to identify an issue, trend, or development. Instead, we need to show what the impacts are, why this is happening or what the opportunities could be.

One of the biggest barriers to producing great inside is the ability to turn a piece of analysis into actionable outputs.

Quite often find that pieces of analysis provide problem-identification and trends. These trends may be a massive breakthrough, but for the business this is not enough. To be of value to the business, insight needs to give us the answers of what needs to happen next. The "**so, what**?"

So, what? is a question regularly asked by very senior stakeholders of insight they receive.

This essential step in insight is one that can be very daunting to data scientists and reporting analysts alike. This is because the work being undertaken in this analysis will have been of a very technical nature. By extending this into a conclusion, the colleague is opening themselves up to argument because of their interpretation of this analysis. This is where we, the managers, need to ensure that the framework and the culture of the team support developing these conclusions.

Should we instead, allow the interpretation of this analysis to be handed over from the data scientists and reporting analysis to the business to undertake, then we will have a significant danger that the business will not fully appreciate how the analysis has been produced or have the same statistical knowledge used in its creation. This decoupling of the different elements of insight can easily lead to erroneous conclusions which are witnessed all too often.

8.6.2 Pre-emptive Insight

When the insight produced cannot lead to any actionable conclusions, instead leading to a description of what is happening, the alternative is to ask why?

Great insight not only answers the question that has been asked, but also pre-empts the next one that will be asked by the recipient of the insight.

As with the advancement of so, what? Insight in the Sect. 8.6.1, creating pre-emptive analysis can be very difficult, and is often avoided by both data scientists and report analysts.

When a piece of analysis has been completed, conclusions drawn and illustrated, the colleague that has created this will often feel that this work is ready for submission. This is only natural. This acts as a barrier to then thinking about what questions will arise from this analysis.

A useful technique to overcoming this is for the data scientist or reporting analyst to prepare this piece of work, and walk it through with a colleague who can then objectively look at the conclusions and ask further questions of this. The most useful usually being "why?"

This question may come in the form of why is this important, or why did this happen? Any and all questions will be useful in thinking through the benefit of the piece of analysis, and what additional questions would be asked by the business.

8.6.3   Impact Analysis

Similar to Sects. 8.6.1 and 8.6.2 is impact analysis. This is analysis to understand the scope of an issue.

For any business to implement a change, there will need to be a thorough understanding of the impact of this change. However, the ways of measuring an impact that the business will consider for this decision will often differ from the measures used in the analysis.

Cost is most commonly a driver for business decisions, though more frequently, customer impacts are playing a role.

What we need to ensure in our insight, is that these metrics are reflected alongside, or instead of metrics that have been used to illustrate the conclusions.

For example, a piece of analysis that looks at the number of complaints made to a company would need to be translated to the cost of this to the business. By reducing the number of complaints, what would the business value be?

Sometimes this translation into metrics that the business will need to make decisions may not be ones the data scientist or reporting analyst are aware of. This is where colleagues with a closer relationship with the relevant stakeholders need to provide support and guidance, and is another example of why collaboration is essential within a team (Sect. 7.2.3).

8.7   Comprehensive Portfolio

8.7.1   Base Reports

Every fact table should have a comprehensive report, based solely on this table (Sect. 5.2). This "**Base Report**" needs to be created whether this has been requested by the business or not.

Whenever a new metric is requested by the business, in addition to including it on the requested report, it should also be included on this base report.

By having a base report, which comes directly from the fact table *(or a view of this)*, we then have a comprehensive and detailed report for which there are a number of benefits:

- Changes to the fact table can be more easily tested and assessed by both report analysts and the business. Changes to other reports.
- Changes to other reports can then be tested by comparing against this base report, rather than having to spend additional time working out what the correct sources should be.
- Confidence in your team from the business will be much higher, that all your reports align when they can easily match between reports.
- Complex metrics which are usually only seen as an overall summary can then be interrogated at a much lower level in this report.
- Ad-hoc requests can be answered immediately with this report, either by having your report analysts extract the numbers, or ideally providing access to it for the business to self-serve.

8.7.2 Aligned Reporting

Having aligned reporting is an essential component of any reporting team. By ensuring this is set up and maintained, this will drive benefits for both your own team and the business.

1. Every report should follow the same colour scheme, naming convention and format.
2. Reports should have the same cover sheet on with information on the purpose of the report, last refresh date, version number, and contact/escalation details.
3. Report identifiers such as a code or assignment at the start of the report name make report identification and report sorting easier.
4. Naming conventions for your reports should be descriptive and obvious.

In combination, these attributes make it very easy to go from one report to the next, immediately understand how to use each report, where to go for certain information and what to expect.

This will make it much easier for not just the business to use the reports, but for your own team to make changes. It will also save a great deal of time in explaining how to use new reports to the business.

Creating a centralised repository or access point for your reporting is another important aspect of your reporting portfolio. This will provide a centralised point of access to your reports, through which access control can be implemented. Additional details of your team, contact and escalation points can be included.

Access to the reports should be in the form of easily managed groups. Access requests can become an onerous part of report management, and in some business environments, this can be made easier using business-controlled groups *(such as active directory groups in Microsoft Windows)*.

Regular maintenance of reporting is essential. When your reporting infrastructure has become full automated (Sect. 6.5), this becomes even more important, as your team will not have day-to-day contact with individual reports. This is easily achieved with weekly and monthly maintenance checks, though you may find the business provide much quicker notification of issues, in which case it is important the contact details for your team are easily obtainable.

8.8 Outsourcing Reporting

Business knowledge creates great reporting and insight. Without this business knowledge, mistakes can and will be made.

Throughout most of the sections in this book, there has been a focus on understanding the business, its challenges, constraints, and upcoming evolution to be able to provide not just a great team, stakeholder relationship, data infrastructure, and comprehensive reporting; but even just an okay one. Even the most basic of reporting functions needs to have a thorough business knowledge.

Because of this, outsourcing large or complex reporting functions will usually not work.

There is a distinction here between large or complex reporting functions, and outsourcing a specific reporting function.

Most applications will have some form of reporting built into them. This will often be in the form of a summary graphic to show you how something is performing, what is left to do, and is usually quite basic.

An example of this is your phone showing you your step count for the day. This reporting will reflect exactly what data is in the tool, using the knowledge of that company's engineers to do so; however, it will not have the knowledge of your specific situation. Your phone will not know what context your step count will have been in. Did you spend the day rowing, put your phone down for part of the day, or has someone else been using your phone as well?

Inbuilt reporting is very common, and useful, if not essential in many applications. However, the context of what these tools report on should always be remembered, and care taken in ensuring we have control of any reporting that requires business knowledge.

For the remainder of this section, we will be discussing the outsourcing of larger and more complex reporting functions than this localised inbuilt reporting capability.

I have been responsible for the in-housing or management of numerous outsourced reporting functions. I have yet to see one that has been relevant to the business and correct. This is not to say that it cannot happen, but there are additional challenges, we will discuss later that are unlikely to be met.

Amongst these failures, have been outsourced reporting systems that have so poorly reflected the business, that hundreds of millions of pounds have been lost, as the reporting was not correctly identifying machines or assets that weren't working, others in which incorrect conclusions have been drawn, which have led to projects and changes being formulated, with no chance of realising these erroneous benefits, wasting great amounts of money, resources, and time, and some of which have led to incorrect regulatory reporting and the potential for severe fines from these regulatory bodies.

8.8.1 The Post Office Horizon Scandal

In 1999, Royal Mail commissioned the company Fujitsu to provide a system to track transactions, accounting and stocktaking. The system they built was called Horizon.

Using the reporting from this Horizon system, the Post Office was able to identify employees that were stealing money from them.

Between 2000 and 2014, the Post Office took 736 sub-postmasters and sub-postmistresses to court and was able to successfully prosecute them for false accounting and theft. Some of these employees were sent to prison and most ruined financially, destroying their lives.

However, Horizon was wrong. It had issues in the way it was calculating its reporting which caused shortfalls in its accounting.

In December 2019, following and lengthy and drawn-out series of civil law cases, the Post Office agreed to pay compensation to 555 of these claimants to the value of £58 million. Further cases have ensued and will continue to do so as more of the original convictions overturned, and compensation sought (Fig. 8.7).

Following the conclusion of this case, the Judge said the system was not "remotely robust" and contained "bugs, errors and defects".

The outsourcing of this system had ruined many employees' lives, cost the business millions, and destroyed the reputation of the Post Office.

Such large-scale applications can and will only succeed when the business is fully aligned with all parts of the project. Everything covered in this book applies equally to these projects as it does to managing an in-house reporting team.

To be comprehensive in our assessment of outsourcing a reporting function, there are several more considerations to discuss:

1. Data quality and reporting accuracy of processes and data manipulation for outsourced reporting become almost impossible to manage by the business, and instead we must have faith in the company to be managing this correctly.
2. Erroneous data being provided to the outsourcing company will have major impacts on their reporting infrastructure, but without control or oversight of how this is being dealt with, the consequences are unknown.
3. Ongoing engagement with stakeholders to keep your reporting proactive and relevant cannot occur.
4. Future proofing your reporting capabilities cannot be achieved easily, and instead must be offered by the company providing the outsourcing.

Fig. 8.7 The Royal Courts of Justice (https://commons.wikimedia.org/wiki/File:Rolls_Building,_
Royal_Courts_of_Justice.jpg)

5. Timescales for changes need to be in line with what the outsourced company can provide, so engagement of this company needs to be well in advance of any business changes, which becomes limiting to the agility and flexibility of your business.
6. To stop using this outsourcing company is a consideration to bear in mind. This will usually involve a large project to provide a replacement service in-house, with related infrastructure and tools.
7. And finally; in most situations, these services are going to have a significant cost. The most difficult for your business to handle will be the cost of requesting changes. As your company is now reliant on this outsourced company, they will have a strong position to warrant increased costs.

This is not to say that all of these hurdles are unsurmountable; they are not. But in order to understand how to achieve an outsourced reporting capability, you must understand the full complexity and breadth of the challenges ahead.

8.9   Outsourcing Insight

Outsourcing insight is becoming increasingly common as tech start-ups and enterprise software companies offer these additional services.

These companies will take data from your organisation which you have prepared for them, or directly from one of your source systems and carry out their own processing, manipulation and data science to present it back to you as a finished product.

Sometimes this can work well, especially when the external company providing your reporting and insight is the same one managing one of your enterprise or third-party systems, but as with outsourcing reporting (Sect. 8.8), there is a distinction between an inbuilt insight function and the complex insight that requires business knowledge. For insight, business knowledge becomes an even more essential part of this process.

Because of the complexity of any valuable business insight, all of the issues and concerns of outsourcing reporting are present and increased for outsourcing insight (Sect. 8.8).

Such outsourcing approaches to reporting come from the misconception that the insight is the difficult part of reporting, for which is clearly incorrect.

8.10 Chapter Summary

1. A key goal of any reporting team is to reduce ad-hoc reporting.
2. Ensure your team works proactively towards your strategy, never on quick-wins.
3. Insight needs to be actionable and pre-emptive.
4. Outsourcing should be fully understood before embarking upon.

References

1. *Fiasco over Covid count.* Ben Spencer (2020) [Daily Mail]
2. *Covid cases 'lost' in test and trace blunder.* Laura Donnelly (2020) [Daily Telegraph]
3. *Tableau.* Tableau Software, LLC https://www.tableau.com
4. *Business Objects.* SAP (2021) https://www.sap.com/uk/products/bi-platform.html
5. *Power BI.* Microsoft (2021) https://powerbi.microsoft.com

Chapter 9
Strategy

9.1 Your Evolved Strategy

Now is time to start developing your complete strategy for the team.

This is a task that should not be taken lightly and can easily take weeks or even months to complete.

Take each goal you have set in your Day 1 strategy, and any more you have developed on the road so far. In turn, consider both the benefits each one of these has for the four elements of a reporting team, and where this goal will fit into your plan.

1. Team (Chaps. 2 and 3)
2. Data (Chaps. 4, 5, and 6)
3. Stakeholders (Chap. 7)
4. Reporting and insight (Chap. 8)

From this, you will be able to build a catalogue of strategic goals we will refer to later.

Now comes the fun part, the puzzle of working out how each goals fits together and how to get from where you are now to the end goal.

In order to create a roadmap of your strategy, we must once again progress through the four elements of a reporting team in turn, to understand how everything can fit together.

9.2 Team Strategy

A useful starting point of creating your team strategy is to think about the roles of each of your team members, how they will interact with each other and with stakeholders, and whether this will change over time.

© The Author(s), under exclusive license to Springer Nature Singapore Pte Ltd. 2025   107
J. Mackay, *From Data to Insights*, https://doi.org/10.1007/978-981-96-3545-0_9

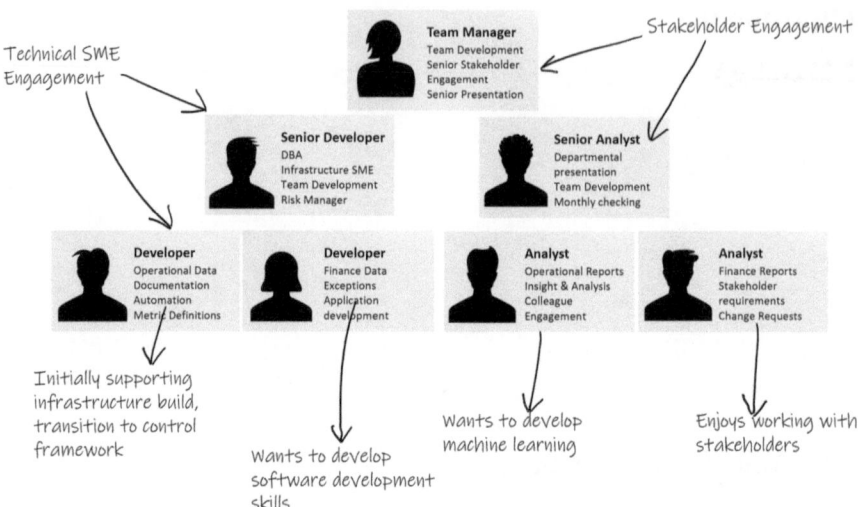

Technical SME
Engagement

Stakeholder Engagement

Team Manager
Team Development
Senior Stakeholder
Engagement
Senior Presentation

Senior Developer
DBA
Infrastructure SME
Team Development
Risk Manager

Senior Analyst
Departmental
presentation
Team Development
Monthly checking

Developer
Operational Data
Documentation
Automation
Metric Definitions

Developer
Finance Data
Exceptions
Application
development

Analyst
Operational Reports
Insight & Analysis
Colleague
Engagement

Analyst
Finance Reports
Stakeholder
requirements
Change Requests

Initially supporting
infrastructure build,
transition to control
framework

Wants to develop
software development
skills

Wants to develop
machine learning

Enjoys working with
stakeholders

Fig. 9.1 Example of a team structure high-level sketch

Visualise your team as it is now, and as it will be throughout your strategy. It is very likely that the type of work your team will be undertaking will change, especially if you are managing a pre-existing team that you want to develop.

Open and honest conversations with your team on what their aspirations are, where they would like to develop and what skills they have will make this possible. Never assume. The most unlikely colleagues often harbour hidden talents and drive that can often be suppressed when the colleague doesn't have the opportunity to use them, or lacks confidence in their own skillset (Fig. 9.1).

Alongside creating the strategy or how your team will develop, this will allow you to create *(if you haven't done so already)*, or develop your individual colleague development plans.

Each stage of your strategy will have different demands for you team (Fig. 9.2).

In the example above, we have shown then transition of skills, assessing which colleagues we will want to develop the skillsets of. This needs to take into consideration the colleague's strengths and desired career progressions.

These conversations aren't easy. Some colleagues will have spent years or even decades working with manual processes, or avoiding liaising with stakeholders. Helping them to see how they can develop their skills and enabling them to work on more rewarding work will be essential here.

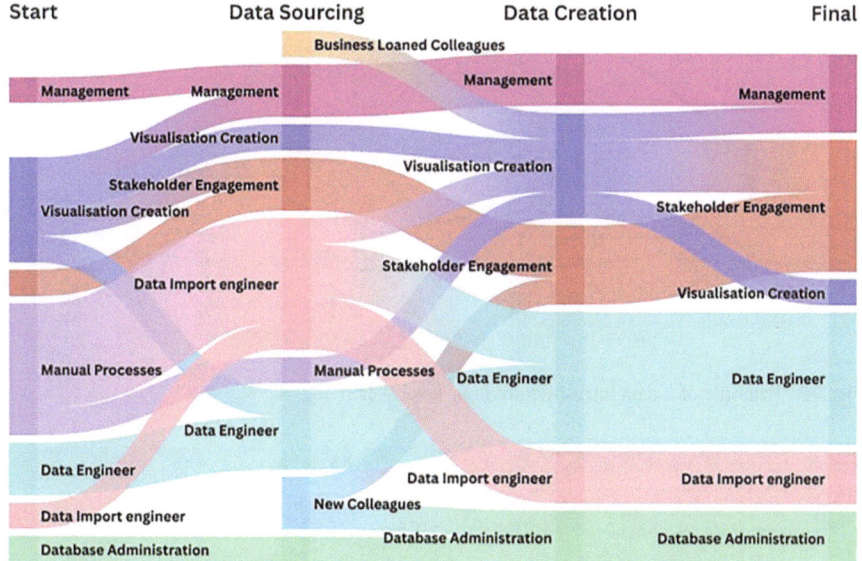

Fig. 9.2 Example of a team demand strategy. (Created with Flourish Studio) [1]

9.3   Data Strategy

Create a list of all the data sources that are going to be used in the infrastructure. Group these together into functional areas, then sketch out how these will fit together.

This will give you an indication of which parts of the infrastructure need developing first, and so the basis of a plan of which needs working on first (Fig. 9.3).

Using this example above, we can see that mapping is required to create the joins between the different systems, and so needs to be early on in the infrastructure development, whilst the combined summary data needs to be left until everything else has been developed.

With this in mind, we can start to plan out how the individual actions of our strategy will fall into place, and which colleagues or team, will be best suited to supporting this (Fig. 9.4).

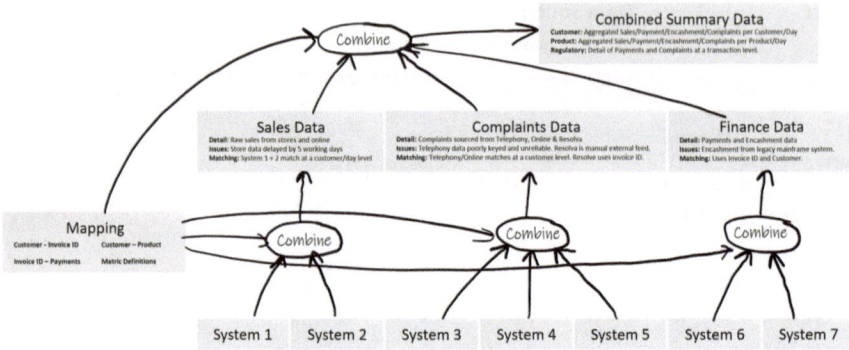

Fig. 9.3 Example of a data infrastructure high-level sketch

Order	Task	Colleague	Dependencies
1	Create Infrastructure Environment	Senior Developer	
2	Bring in data from System 1	Any Developer	Task 1
3	Bring in data from System 2	Any Developer	Task 1
4	Bring in data from System 3	Any Developer	Task 1
5	Bring in data from System 4	Any Developer	Task 1
6	Bring in data from System 5	Any Developer	Task 1
7	Bring in data from System 6	Any Developer	Task 1
8	Bring in data from System 7	Any Developer	Task 1
9	Create Mapping Framework	Senior Developer	Tasks 1-8
10	Combine System1,2 data into Sales Data	Any Developer	Task 9
11	Combine System3,4,5 data into Complaint Data	Any Developer	Task 9
12	Combine System6,7 data into Finance Data	Any Developer	Task 9
13	Create Combined Summary Data	Senior Developer	Tasks 10-12

Fig. 9.4 Example of first draft of data tasks

This can then be worked through with the team to fill in detail for each step, work out what other dependencies exist for each one, which in turn will need support from other team members, teams, stakeholders, or suppliers (Fig. 9.5).

Every element from the Chaps. 3 and 4 of this book and our strategy need to be applied to this list.

This document will provide the basis for your work allocation, team assignment and progress reporting throughout the development of your team, so it is essential this document is kept fully up to date, and also that you maintain a version control over it, so any amendments by your team can be checked against previous views further down the road.

As the team strategy progresses, it is likely that you will need to make constant updates, add in new tasks and dependencies as the development evolves. Ensure that your team refers back to this document on a regular basis, and this process will become easier.

Order	Task	Owner	Dependencies
10	Combine System1,2 data into Sales Data	Senior Developer	Tasks 1-9
10.1	Investigate which values between system 1,2 required for join	Senior Developer	Tasks 1-9
10.2	Discussion with stakeholders to understand values in system 1	Senior Analyst	Task 10.1
10.3	Discussion with stakeholders to understand values in system 2	Senior Analyst	Task 10.1
10.4	Create joins between system 1,2	Senior Developer	Tasks 10.1-10.2
10.5	Test Joins	Any Developer	Task 10.4
10.6	Provide draft view of combined data between system 1,2 for testing	Senior Analyst	Task 10.5
10.7	Stakeholder to provide feedback	Senior Analyst	Stakeholders
10.8	Build joins between system 1,2	Senior Developer	Task 10.8
10.9	Create combined Sales Data table	Senior Developer	Task 10.8

Fig. 9.5 Example of expansion of data tasks

9.4 Stakeholder Strategy

Much of the work initially engaging with your stakeholders will need to precede the work your team will carry out on the data infrastructure.

However, the data infrastructure tasks need to be defined before you engage fully with your stakeholders, so your team can anticipate what questions to ask and provide expectations on both what your team will be working on, and what inputs they will need to provide.

Requirements gathering and testing can often take much longer than you first anticipate. Your stakeholders will *(hopefully)* not want to make mistakes and may require input from a wide selection of colleagues. Operational and business priorities may take precedence over supporting your team, which is something you may have to manage.

Tasks that are presented to your stakeholders that appear too complex may cause issues with your stakeholders due to a lack of understanding. Because of this, it is always best to walk through more complex questions collaboratively with stakeholders where possible, and break down your questions into fragments that are easier for them to respond to.

Stakeholders may have an expectation that they will not be involved in your team's strategy. As described in detail throughout the Chap. 7, you need to ensure this is not the case, and your stakeholders are working with your team collaboratively throughout your team's development.

As described in the Sect. 7.2.4, engagement with your stakeholders becomes much easier when visualisations and outputs are provided to stakeholders when you are asking questions of them.

The same applies when seeking feedback on existing processes and reporting. When we are asking for feedback, which could well be negative, it is much better to demonstrate alternatives that will be able to mitigate the current issues.

We can expect our different stakeholders to have very different challenges, relating to how they use our reporting, tools, and processes (Fig. 9.6).

Senior Management

Current Reporting Feedback: Unhappy with reliability of reporting. Questions raised over inconsistency between reports.

Future Requirements: Would like to have interactive reports to drill down to lower levels. Wants to see more insight incorporated into packs.

Operations

Current Reporting Feedback: Unhappy with communications of reporting and system issues.

Future Requirements: Would like reporting ready earlier each day, for when the first telephony shift starts at 7am. Want to be able to track how each colleague is performing.

Finance

Current Reporting Feedback: Happy with current reporting.

Future Requirements: They are currently transforming the reporting they receive into other summaries. Would like this work to be done for them.

Fig. 9.6 Example of feedback from stakeholders

Because of these differences, we may decide to approach each set of stakeholders in different ways and will require feedback at different points in our strategy.

In our initial meetings with stakeholders, we will also be looking to find out what reports they want, though as discussed in Sect. 8.2, what they want and need is often not the same. This can be another time in which showing them how comprehensive, and detailed reporting can answer several questions at once and pre-empt future questions (Fig. 9.7).

This collaboration with our stakeholders will allow us to build an initial reporting suite list.

What we need to pay special attention to, is any data we may not have in scope for our data infrastructure already, or any functionality not catered for yet. Elements like this will need to be inserted as close to the start of our task list as possible.

This can be difficult to identify all of the requirements from these initial calls, and this is where we need to stop thinking of how a report might look, and instead only focus on what is going into it and how it will be used.

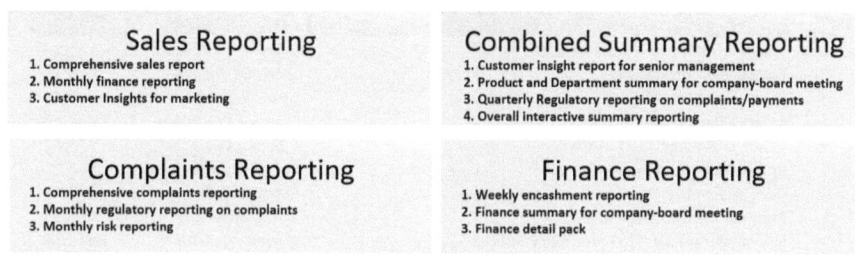

Fig. 9.7 Example of a reporting suite draft

A simple request such as "a stakeholder wanting different departments seeing different versions of the report", so a report can dynamically refresh with the appropriate departmental data, would require a complete rework of your data infrastructure is not spotted early enough.

This is why I cannot stress the importance of enough, it is essential that you, the manager, understands enough about the data infrastructure and reporting tools, to realise the implications of the requirements. This was discussed in Sect. 2.3.

9.5   Reporting Strategy

Reporting should be developed using *agile* methodology (Sect. 7.3.2).

A good report will have many different components to it, and each one will have different dependencies and inputs to it. Many of these components will require work being undertaken by our engineers or changes to the infrastructure and all will require stakeholder feedback.

Because of this, the components of a report need segmenting into separate tasks, to facilitate effective development.

We need to consider which elements of a report will be generic across our reporting, and which will be specific to just one report.

For example, whilst the information being provided in a definitions tab may be specific to that one report, we may want this information to be stored on our server, so we can update definitions dynamically through a mapping tool.

This dynamic-definition element will have several tasks split across our strategy, which we can insert into our task list appropriately (Fig. 9.8).

As you can see in this example, the quickest we can start working on the definitions' framework is step 4, very early in our task list, and far in advance of creating our first reports. When this task has been completed, we can then seek inputs from our stakeholders on the definitions of the metrics being used in their associated reports.

Order	Task	Colleague	Dependencies
1	Create Infrastructure Environment	Senior Developer	
2	Bring in data from System 1	Any Developer	Task 1
3	Bring in data from System 2	Any Developer	Task 1
4	Create Mapping Framework	Senior Developer	Tasks 2-3
5	Create Definitions Framework	Senior Developer	Task 4
6	Bring in data from System 3	Any Developer	Task 1
7	Bring in data from System 4	Any Developer	Task 1
8	Bring in data from System 5	Any Developer	Task 1
9	Link in systems 3,4,5 to mapping,definitions	Senior Developer	Tasks 6-8
10	Bring in data from System 6	Any Developer	Task 1
11	Bring in data from System 7	Any Developer	Task 1
12	Link in systems 6,7 to mapping,definitions	Senior Developer	Tasks 10-11
13	Combine System1,2 data into Sales Data	Any Developer	Task 4
14	Create Sales Report 1: Sales Detail	Any Analyst	Tasks 4,5
15	Create Sales Report 2	Any Analyst	Tasks 4,5
16	Create Sales Report 3	Any Analyst	Tasks 4,5
17	Create Sales Report 4	Any Analyst	Tasks 4,5
18	Create Sales Report 5	Any Analyst	Tasks 4,5

Fig. 9.8 Example of integration of dynamic definitions into task list

9.6 The Journey

As we are starting to see in building the *reporting strategy* (Sect. 9.5), the various tasks associated with *team*, *data*, *stakeholders* and *reporting and insight* all interlink and create a mesh of dependencies (Chaps. 3, 4, 5, 6, 7, and 8).

By maintaining a focus on keeping our task list comprehensive and up to date, we can be certain that the progression of the tasks is logical. We can also ensure that tasks are placed as early in the progression of our strategy as possible.

The next thing we will need to assess is which colleagues will be available to work on which tasks.

This will enable us to understand the workload of the team throughout the implementation of our strategy, potential bottlenecks, and importantly for our stakeholders, a timeline from which we can set expectations.

A typical tool we use in *project management* to assess a project's flow is through the use of a Gantt chart (Sect. 7.3; Fig. 9.9).

From this initial template, we can then see where we can have tasks running concurrently, and so utilise our team's capacity.

As we include more of the tasks into this Gantt chart, the complexity will grow as we get closer to a comprehensive project plan.

There will be many elements of your team that are independent of this project plan, such as holiday planners, personal development plans, colleague engagement activities, and learning new skills. All of these can be used to plug the gaps in your teams' activities and ensure a constant workload.

Using this project plan, you will be able to populate estimated completion dates of activities on your task list from which you can then track progress within your team, and also start to communicate estimated delivery dates for the various elements of your strategy with stakeholders and senior management.

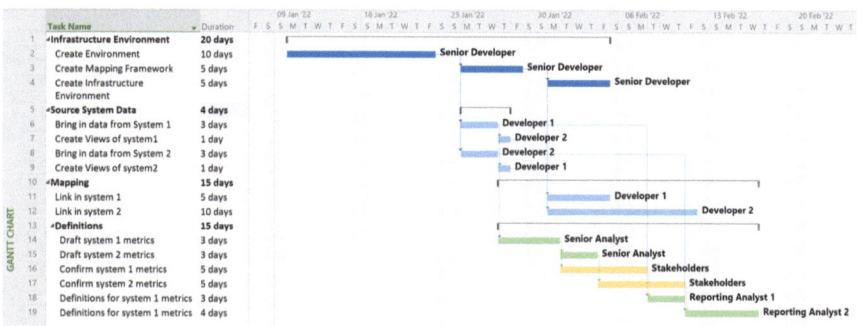

Fig. 9.9 Example Gantt chart

Though your strategy is now complete, and your team able to work through the relevant actions in the most logical and efficient order, you should expect changes to arise.

It would be extremely rare not to see requirements change, challenges arise and businesses develop as your strategy unfolds. These changes each need to be carefully considered and accommodated within your plans. However, you will be in the best possible place to adapt to these challenges and ensure your strategy succeeds.

9.7   Chapter Summary

1. Build a catalogue starting with your day 1 strategy, and incorporating goals relevant to you for the elements of Team, Data, Stakeholders, Reporting, and Insight.
2. Create a map of how your team will develop throughout the implementation of your strategy.
3. Create a map of the data sources and build draft architecture lists and diagrams.
4. Stakeholder takes time, and it is essential that they are involved in the creation of your strategy.
5. Integrate the list of reporting to build into your list of strategic tasks. Build projects plan from this completed list.
6. Keep on reviewing your strategy whilst and after it has been delivered. The needs of the business will always keep on evolving.

Reference

1. *Flourish Studio*. Sankey Diagram created with Flourish https://flourish.studio

Chapter 10
Conclusion

What does the future of data analytics look like?

The scope of these teams is evolving. Not all that long ago, reporting teams worked on largely manual processes, creating files and slides to be sent out regularly.

Automation transformed the infrastructure of these teams and the work they carried out. It remained a buzzword for a decade as companies slowly embraced the technology. At the same time, a battle took place between the visualisation tools, which still rages to this day, even if the tools are largely converging to provide the same functionality and features.

Cloud technologies have become the bright new future to ever-growing datasets, and the companies producing these try to lure us into their eco-systems with a promise of simplicity. Data science came along with machine learning (ML) initially, and tortuous hours spent building data models, then libraries to replace much of this work. Artificial Intelligence (AI) emerged as the latest catchphrase, though it was revamped with the inception of the generative AI proliferating services and products today.

AI is transforming not only data analytics, but business in general. To fully understand its impact, we must understand exactly what it is to be a data analyst.

The heart of data analytics is data visualisation. It is the end product of the data analytics team.

Without a way of visualising data, data is largely useless to humans. A computer or phone is just a device that translates data into outputs we can understand. It shows us text and images and plays audio, and each one requires us to interact with each output to make this data productive.

We provide the feedback loop for the device to identify what to do next by reacting to it. This is the part of the process humans are phenomenal at, being the feedback loop for the machine.

This is why data visualisation is such an essential part of any company that deals with data. We verify everything we see, validating, spotting issues or opportunities. The better the visualisations, the more we can do.

J. Mackay, *From Data to Insights*, https://doi.org/10.1007/978-981-96-3545-0_10

Now consider AI and the outputs it provides. AI uses algorithms and computational models to identify patterns in data, make predictions, and generate responses based on those predictions. Critically for AI, this output is a prediction and lacks a feedback loop for the AI to check the veracity of its output. We can parse the outputs multiple times through the AI, even using different models. This may reduce the rate of errors, but they will still exist.

When we are building AI into processes or products, just as we require humans to interact with computers and phones through data visualisations, we need to remember to include humans in the feedback loop for AI.

AI has become a powerful tool for delivering our data strategy. Just remember, that if all you have is a hammer, everything looks like a nail, and the same is true for AI.

Throughout this book, we have discussed the many elements that make up a data analytics team, each part being a cog in the machine that AI will also fit into. Its effectiveness in the data strategy depends on thoughtful implementation. Whilst we will need to embrace the benefits it brings; we must recognise the irreplaceable role the human plays in validating and refining outputs.

The same balance we needed to achieve with task automation, stakeholder engagement, data consistency, validation, and quality is the same balance we need to ensure with AI.

Through each step data analytics has made since its inception, the value of what the data analytics team can deliver has continued to increase. Never has data analytics been so essential and central to the requirements of business, and this trend is continuing.

This is a great time to be at the forefront of data analytics, as we stand at the cusp of unprecedented opportunities to harness the combined power of data, AI, and human expertise.